©   **Verlag Zabert Sandmann GmbH, Munich**
First edition 1999

Concept/Recipes:	Werner Meisinger
Editor:	Gertrud Köhn
	Angelika Schlenk
Graphic Design/DTP:	Michael Knoch
	Georg Feigl
Translator:	Kathy Tolson for Textra Fachübersetzungen GmbH
Photos:	Alexander Haselhoff (Features)
	Christian R. Schulz (Recipes)
Kitchen Assistance:	Peter Buchegger
	Maria Reiter
Production:	Peter Karg-Cordes
Lithography:	inteca Media Service GmbH,
	Rosenheim
Printing:	OAN – a member of Interdruck
	Graphischer Großbetrieb GmbH,
	Leipzig
ISBN:	3-932023-51-X

RUDOLF & KARL OBAUER

THE NEW *Austrian* COOKBOOK

More than 100 classic dishes and new creations

Photos by
Alexander Haselhoff and Christian Schulz

ZS
ZABERT
SANDMANN

Contents

The Country and its Cuisine

Year after year, millions of visitors come to Austria to admire the wonderful scenery and experience the culture and the many festivals, but equally to enjoy the typical methods of cooking here. The Austrians themselves are very much conscious of what good eating and cooking means. They say "Good food keeps body and soul together." What could be more important? This book has been written in praise of Austrian cuisine, a strikingly diverse cuisine considering the small dimensions of the country. And a pleasingly modern, inspired cuisine when the right chefs are behind the dishes.

Karl and Rudolf Obauer, the authors of this book, definitely number among the most stimulating interpreters of Austria's good cuisine. They are even able to give hints and tips on how to prepare great classics to lend them that extra appetizing touch.

The spectrum of specialties and delightful treats Austria offers is truly remarkable and mirrors the contrasting landscapes, ranging from upper Alpine regions down to deep lowlands in Burgenland that extend far into Hungary. The Styrian hills roll in long undulations toward the mild south and, in contrast, a raw wind blows for most of the year on the high plateau of Waldviertel. Each region has its own microclimate to promote the flourishing agricultural products typical of each area. The Marchfeld plain north-east of Vienna is renowned for its asparagus, in southern Styria – and virtually only there – pumpkins are cultivated for the production of oil from their seeds, and many varieties of poppy grow in Waldviertel. Naturally, each of these regions is proud of its own particular method of cooking.

Melange of regional Cuisines

If anyone mentions Austrian cuisine, he means a melange of countless, very characteristic regional cuisines. Consequently, many theoretical gastronomes maintain, "There isn't an Austrian cuisine just as there isn't a general Chinese cuisine," and in fact, the stuffed peppers of Burgenland and the cheese spaetzle of Vorarlberg are no smaller culinary worlds apart than Cantonese fish soup and a Mongolian fire pot. The hard mountain and piquant cheeses indispensable for Vorarlberg's pasta are something Burgenland peoples have perhaps just heard of; the paprika powder and pureed tomato peppers so popular on the Pannonian side of Austria are looked upon as more exotic ingredients in Vorarlberg. These are just a few of numerous other examples of the wide spectrum Austrian cuisine encompasses. The famous pancakes, for example, play a major role in Vienna's dessert specialties and are often enjoyed as a main course in the eastern parts of Austria, yet in other regions they are not particularly popular. The Viennese lose the advantage they have with their pastries and desserts over

Culinary delights direct from the source: Trout for Obauer specialties are reared not far from Werfen.

Landscapes leave their marks on peoples and cuisine.

other Austrians when it comes to fish. For this, Salzkammergut serves up dozens of ideas. In Carinthia, cheese or meat spaetzle enjoys the status of an indisputable luxury and staple food, but elsewhere in Austria, noodles are rarely prepared in this way.

FROM OKRA TO SOY SAUCE – NEW INGREDIENTS, NEW SPICES

This book presents the most attractive aspects of Austrian cuisine. The recipes comprise everything from great classics and regional specialties to totally surprising ideas; from the best way to prepare Wiener Schnitzel through to chicken turnovers with tomato sauce. Ingredients that have become well-known or popular here in recent years are used to complement conventional ones. Never has there been such a wide range of vegetables, fish, herbs and spices available as today. This variety should be exploited to the full!

The best ways to combine soy sauce, balsamic vinegar, fresh basil, oyster and shiitake mushrooms, arugola or cherry tomatoes with conventional ingredients of the Austrian cuisine are illustrated in this book. Simmered calves' tongues, for example, go excellently with okra, a vegetable that has been sorely ignored in Austrian cookbooks (see recipe on page 141).

Give game sauce an extra-special spicy touch by adding ginger (page 112). Turnovers – or should we say ravioli – filled with ricotta are the perfect addition to a spring herb soup (turn to page 42).

New ingredients are employed in a simple and uncomplicated way in this book to enhance the taste and heighten the pleasure of cooking. That is why it is called The New Austrian Cookbook. However, a new cuisine, a culinary revolution, such as the Nouvelle Cuisine, is not what is intended. The Austrian cuisine has survived well without a revolution. What gives this book its particular fascination is the elegant fusion of traditional specialties with inspiration from different and exotic cuisines. Borders are vanishing in cooking, too, eating habits are changing more rapidly than ever; nowadays, culinary development advances with breathtaking speed.

It took only very few years for dishes like tiramisu, mozzarella and tomatoes or sweet and sour pork to establish themselves on many Austrian menus. It is simple to think of similar delicious compositions with a little taste and imagination. Karl and Rudolf Obauer, for example, came up with "chicken with ginger and soy wrapped in rice," "salsify gratin" or "char with kohlrabi and lime sauce."

Harvest time is preserving time. Apart from pear, cherry and apple compote, the Obauer brothers also make specialties like buckthorn compote.

Cold-smoked, eaten warm. Smoked trout is also an ideal filling for pancakes.

The seeds for the famous Styrian pumpkin-seed oil have to be immaculate.

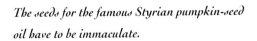

9

IMPROVISATION AS A WAY TO SUCCESS

This New Austrian Cookbook ultimately promotes the contemporary art of omission. The two authors demonstrate how: They have limited the number of ingredients to very few in many dishes, following the principle that a simple recipe can be delightful and imaginative. One of the most simple dishes consists of potatoes, grappa and caviar. They can be prepared in a flash and charm even the critical palate of gourmets. No other ingredient could make the grappa potato more delicious. And, on top of this, the art of omission is useful when interpreting lists of ingredients

Farmers are the chefs' most important partners in attaining a tasty cuisine.

"Always look for what's good!" – The Obauer brothers taste Tyrolean schnapps distilled by Günter Rochelt (left).

that tend to be rather extensive. Where several types of vinegar, different sorts of oil or numerous herbs and spices head a recipe, they are only to be understood as recommendations. It would be ideal if everything in these long lists could be easily obtained. But it is not absolutely necessary. As everyone knows, improvisation is a well-proven way to success in good cuisine.

Even with all the inspiration in the world – cooking remains a skill. Karl Obauer positions passion-fruit mousse.

A country molds its cuisine. A good cuisine is almost always regional.

Karl and Rudolf Obauer

The brothers Karl and Rudolf Obauer are well known for their extremely tasty cuisine. Their restaurant and hotel in Werfen (Salzburg) has been awarded supreme honors by culinary critics. The unmistakable style of the Obauers' cuisine is marked by concentration on the essential. But flavor is a priority. Karl and Rudolf Obauer restrict themselves to ingredients of choice quality and obtain many of them from farmers in their direct vicinity. The ponds providing the Obauers with salmon and salmon trout are only a few minutes' walk away, nestled in an idyllic forest. Free-range eggs come from a local mountain farmer. Products from large-scale livestock farming do not cross their doorstep. On principle, but also because the meat from naturally reared animals is of optimum flavor. Good flavor for Karl and Rudolf Obauer does not mean luxurious ingredients. They often serve truffles and caviar in their restaurant, but the brothers also know the secret of producing delicacies from everyday ingredients. They unfold new exciting dimensions for familiar dishes with imagination and creativity. The Obauer trout strudel, for instance, could be understood as a further development of "salmon in pastry", but it is far more refined in flavor. "Oxtail with potato puree" sounds very much like a traditional dish, but when Karl and Rudolf Obauer interpret it, the result becomes the highlight of a culinary occasion ...

> "Congratulations to the Obauer brothers who, with great sensitivity, present the art of cooking in its most attractive form. Their recipes always relate to the roots of the region, yet fulfil all the criteria demanded by modern cuisine."
>
> **Paul Bocuse**

The two brothers learned their trade in first-class restaurants at home and abroad. In addition, Rudolf Obauer pursued his culinary studies in France, where he cooked with exceptional gastronomic artists, like Jean and Pierre Troisgros, Alain Chapel and Emile Jung.

Today, Karl and Rudolf Obauer still travel regularly to the top-class award-winning gourmet restaurants – for they have long been two of today's great chefs. A personal affinity takes them to Eastern Asia time and time again, where they gather additional inspiration for their cuisine.

Hors d'Œuvres

PRELUDE AND CULINARY MINIATURES

Ricotta and Asparagus Terrine

Ingredients for 15 portions

1 lb asparagus

3/4 oz butter

1 lb ricotta

30 leaves of wild garlic

3 1/2 oz dried tomatoes

2 tablespoons freshly chopped herbs

Balsamic vinegar and olive oil for sprinkling

Mixed herbs (optional, see page 21)

For the jelly:

2 cups chicken stock

4 tablespoons dry vermouth (e. g. Noilly Prat)

2 tablespoons pectin powder or 7 pieces

of gelatin

Salt

Pepper

For 3 jars of tomato compote, each containing

1 generous cup:

4 1/2 lb beef tomatoes

5 shallots

1 small bunch of mint

4 tablespoons refined sugar

1 teaspoon coriander seeds

1/2 cup dry vermouth

Salt

Pepper

1. Peel the asparagus, cut off the hard ends and boil it in salted water with the butter for 15 minutes.

2. Add the vermouth to the chicken stock and boil, stir in the pectin powder (if using pieces of gelatin, soak these first in cold water and then squeeze them out), season with salt and pepper. Allow the liquid to cool.

3. Mix the ricotta with 1/2 cup of jelly.

4. Place a terrine mold (12 inches long, 4 inches wide) in iced water. Pour a little jelly into the mold. Dip the wild garlic leaves in the jelly and line the mold. Put half of the ricotta into the mold, smoothen, lay half of the cooked asparagus on top and cover with jelly. Add a layer of dried tomatoes. Layer the rest of the ricotta and asparagus alternately in the mold and finish with wild garlic leaves and jelly. Refrigerate the terrine for 3 hours before serving.

5. For the compote: Core the stem ends of the tomatoes, slit the skin crosswise and lay them in boiling water for about 5 seconds. Lift out, rinse with cold water and skin. Halve the tomatoes, remove the flesh and squeeze out the juice.

6. Peel the shallots and cut finely. Chop the tomato flesh coarsely. Wash the mint and pat dry. Braise the tomato flesh with the juice, shallots, mint sprigs, sugar, crushed coriander seeds, vermouth, salt and pepper in the oven at 350 °F for about 1/2 hour.

7. Put the tomato compote into sterile jars.

8. Turn the terrine upside down and remove the mold. Cut into slices and garnish with tomato compote, olive oil, balsamic vinegar and fresh herbs. Perhaps sprinkle over a mixture of herbs.

K. and R. Obauer

The tomato compote is an ideal accompaniment to salads, molds, steamed fish, butter sauces or as "sugo" for pasta of all kinds.

Goat-Cheese Tart with Anchovies

Ingredients for 6 servings

9 oz puff pastry

Olive oil

4 tomatoes

7 oz goat's cream cheese

20 anchovy fillets

For the mixed herbs:

2 teaspoons crushed dried mugwort

2 teaspoons crushed dried marjoram

2 teaspoons fenugreek

1/4 teaspoon dried sage

1. Grease a baking tray (8 x 12 inches) with olive oil. Roll out the pastry to 1/10 inch thickness, lay it on the tray and prick with a fork several times. Preheat the oven to 420 °F.

2. Cut the tomatoes into segments. Scatter the tomatoes, goat's cheese and anchovy fillets on the pastry, sprinkle generously with olive oil and mixed herbs. Bake for approx. 15 minutes.

3. Cut the cake into pieces and serve warm. Salad is an ideal accompaniment.

K. and R. Obauer

Only a small quantity of the mixed herbs given here is needed for sprinkling the tart. The remainder can be stored for a long time in tightly closed jars and is ideal for enhancing mixed salads, rabbit, roast chicken or lamb.

Sour Kid

Ingredients for 10 to 15 servings

2 lb meat from a goat kid (breast, neck, shoulder)

5 1/2 oz carrots

11 oz onions

3 cloves of garlic

2 oz dried tomatoes

1/2 oz curing salt

1 pinch of ground cumin

1 pinch of saffron

Generous 4 cups white wine

1 tablespoon vinegar concentrate

2 teaspoons pectin

1 tablespoon mixed herbs (see left)

Salt

1. Peel the carrots, onions and garlic and grind them together with the meat.

2. Stir in the remaining ingredients (except for the jelly powder and mixed herbs). Simmer for about 1/2 hour, stirring frequently. Stir in the mixed herbs and the jelly powder.

3. Put the mixture into a mold or preserving jars and poach in the oven at 350 °F in a bain-marie.

4. Serve garnished with spring herbs, vegetables and salad (cress, dandelion, wild garlic, young lettuce, asparagus, kohlrabi). Marinate herbs and vegetables with pumpkin-seed oil and cider vinegar.

K. and R. Obauer

The marinade tastes best with an cider-balsamic vinegar from the Gölles distillery (Riegersburg in Styria).

Pumpkin Cannelloni

Ingredients for 8 servings

1 lb pumpkin, preferably Hokkaido pumpkin

1 twig of rosemary

11 oz noodle dough (see right)

3 1/2 oz butter

3 1/2 oz Parmesan cheese

1/2 cup fresh cream

Salt · Pepper

1. Peel the pumpkin and cut off 16 slices that are as thin as possible. Bring the slices of pumpkin to a boil with the rosemary and a little water. Take out of the water and lay aside.

2. Put the remaining pumpkin (approx. 12 oz) into a pan with the butter, cover and steam. Puree the pumpkin, season with salt, pepper and chopped rosemary to taste.

3. Roll out the noodle dough until thin and cut into 6 x 4 inches slices. Boil the noodle slices briefly in salted water, drain and blanche with cold water.

4. Preheat the oven to 480 °F. Place the noodle slices on buttered baking trays. Lay one slice of pumpkin on each, spread with pumpkin puree and shape into rolls. Sprinkle with grated Parmesan cheese and bake for about 5 minutes in the preheated oven.

5. Heat the fresh cream and salt slightly. Put two cannelloni onto each plate. Pour the cream over the cannelloni and sprinkle with Parmesan cheese.

K. and R. Obauer

*Gourmets' hearts will beat faster
if you spread chopped truffles on
the cannelloni before serving.*

Noodle Dough

Ingredients for 6 servings

12 oz semolina

5 1/2 oz flour

4 eggs

3 egg yolks

1 dash of olive oil

1. Mix the ingredients, preferably with the dough hook of a mixer, into a firm, smooth dough.

2. Cover dough with plastic wrap and allow to rest for 1 hour.

3. Roll the dough out thinly using a pasta maker. Sprinkle with semolina each time before rolling.

4. Cut the noodles into the shape required and boil immediately.

K. and R. Obauer

*Do not salt the dough.
If salted dough is not used immediately,
it turns a grayish colour.*

23

Tomatoes with Turkey and Anchovy Cream

Ingredients for 8 servings

9 oz turkey breast

4 beef tomatoes

2 oz cauliflower

3 oz porcini mushrooms

5 anchovy fillets

1/2 crushed garlic clove

1/2 cup milk

1/2 cup fresh cream

1 1/2 oz hard cheese

1 teaspoon anchovy paste

2 tablespoons butter

1/2 tablespoon hot mustard

1 tablespoon peanut oil

1 tablespoon olive oil

1 dash balsamic vinegar

1 to 2 tablespoons fresh, chopped herbs

(e.g. cress, fennel green)

Sugar

Salt

Pepper

1. Slit the skin of the tomatoes, cut out the stalk and put briefly into boiling water. Rinse in cold water, skin, cut into halves vertically and scoop out the flesh.

2. Pick over and wash the cauliflower and porcini and dice with the turkey breast. Simmer with the anchovy fillets and garlic in the milk and cream for 1/2 hour.

3. Grate the cheese. Put the cheese, anchovy paste, butter, hot mustard and peanut oil into the meat and vegetable mixture. Puree in a mixer, add salt and pepper to taste. Spread the cream inside the halved tomatoes.

4. Press the flesh from the tomatoes through a sieve. Mix the juice obtained with olive oil, balsamic vinegar and herbs, add sugar, salt and pepper and pour over the stuffed tomatoes.

K. and R. Obauer

*Serve the tomatoes
with toasted white bread or pesto bread
and sprinkle with fennel green.*

Veal in Swiss Chard

Ingredients for 8 servings

1 1/2 hard white rolls

1 carrot

1 lemon

11 oz shoulder of veal, finely ground

1/2 cup fresh cream

2 egg whites

About 1 1/2 oz butter

Dark breadcrumbs

8 Swiss chard leaves

For the vinaigrette:

6 tablespoons olive oil

6 tablespoons kernel oil

6 tablespoons balsamic vinegar

4 coriander seeds

Juice of 1 lemon

1 teaspoon sugar

Salt

Pepper

1. Grate the crust from the rolls and grate the rolls coarsely. Peel the carrot and cut finely. Grate off the lemon zest. Mix the grated rolls, carrot, lemon zest, ground veal, cream and egg whites and let stand for 1/4 hour.

2. Preheat the oven to 400 °C.

3. Grease eight soufflé molds with butter, sprinkle over the dark breadcrumbs and line them with the Swiss chard leaves. Pour in the mixture. Place the ends of the Swiss chard leaves over the top and brush with melted butter. Cook in the preheated oven for 10 to 15 minutes.

4. For the vinaigrette: Mix the olive oil, kernel oil, balsamic vinegar, crushed coriander, lemon juice, sugar, salt and pepper.

5. Turn out the stuffed Swiss chard leaves, pour over the vinaigrette and serve.

K. and R. Obauer

Asparagus is an ideal accompaniment.

Sardines with Herb Crumbs and Limes

Ingredients for 4 servings

16 sardines

10 basil leaves

5 mint leaves

1 lovage leaf

1 tablespoon pinions

1/2 clove of garlic

1/2 lime

5 to 8 tablespoons olive oil

Small amount of white breadcrumbs

Balsamic vinegar

1. Twist off the heads of the sardines, cut open the stomach, remove the gut, bones and backbone with your fingers.

2. Finely crush the basil leaves, mint leaves, lovage leaf, pinions, garlic, lime zest with olive oil with a pestle and mortar. Stir in a small amount of white breadcrumbs.

3. Lay half of the sardines on their backs, spread the mixture over them and put another sardine on top of each to form a "double" sardine. Preheat the oven to 400 °F.

4. Brush the baking tray with olive oil, lay the sardines on the tray, sprinkle with olive oil and bake for 6 to 8 minutes.

5. Lay the sardines on plates, sprinkle over the lime juice and balsamic vinegar. Steamed young potatoes go well with these.

Smoked trout cream with Fennel Green

Ingredients for 8 servings

2 smoked trout

4 tablespoons sour cream

2 tablespoons crème fraîche

A pinch of cayenne pepper

Fennel green to garnish

3 oz caviar, red salmon roe or trout roe

White or dark bread

1. Remove the bones from the smoked trout. Mix the meat with sour cream, crème fraîche and cayenne pepper.

2. Put the mixture into teacups. Lay the caviar on top and garnish with fennel green. Serve with toasted white or dark bread.

Onions Stuffed with Pheasant Mousse

Ingredients for 8 servings

7 oz pheasant (meat from 2 legs)

1 1/2 oz celeriac

1/2 clove of garlic

1/2 cup milk

1 cup fresh cream

1/2 cup dry sherry

1 juniper berry

1 oz hard cheese

2 tablespoons butter

1/2 tablespoon peanut oil

1/2 tablespoon hot mustard

1/2 cup crème fraîche

8 large onions

Generous amount of sunflower oil for frying

Balsamic vinegar for sprinkling

Salt

Pepper

1. Cut the pheasant meat and celeriac into small pieces, peel the clove of garlic and cut into thin slices.

2. Bring the milk, half of the cream and the sherry to a boil with the juniper berry, add salt and pepper. Add the pheasant meat, celeriac and garlic and simmer for about 1/2 hour.

3. Grate the cheese. Put the cheese, butter, peanut oil, hot mustard and crème fraîche into the pan with the meat. Puree with a hand blender and allow to cool.

4. Whip the remaining cream and fold into the mousse.

5. Put the unpeeled onions into a pan and add enough sunflower oil to cover them (the onions should be close together or too much oil is needed). Simmer the onions in the oil for about 45 minutes. The onions have to be soft; prick with a fork to test.

6. Remove the onions from the fat, peel them. The peel can later be used as a garnish. Cut off the tops and scoop out the flesh inside.

7. Put the pheasant mousse into the onions and cool before serving.

8. Put the filled onions on plates, garnish with onion skin, sprinkle with balsamic vinegar and season with freshly ground salt and pepper.

K. and R. Obauer

Smoked meat enhances the filled onions. They harmonize particularly well with smoked venison.

Marinated Beef Tenderloin with Asparagus and Limes

Ingredients for 4 servings

12 asparagus stalks of thumb thickness

1 teaspoon sugar

14 oz beef tenderloin

4 tablespoons olive oil

3 limes

2 tablespoons soy sauce

Lettuce (e.g. arugola or dandelion)

A little liquid honey

2 oz grated hard cheese

Salt

Pepper

1. Wash and peel the asparagus, cut off the ends and tie into two bundles. Boil in water with sugar and salt until cooked but still firm, rinse in ice water.

2. Cut the tenderloin into fine slices. Mix the olive oil, juice from the limes and soy sauce. Dip the tenderloin into the marinade.

3. Place the asparagus and tenderloin on four plates and sprinkle the marinade over these. Garnish with greens, sprinkle with a little honey, grated cheese and black pepper.

Ox-Lip Terrine

Ingredients for 4 to 8 servings

1 lb ox lip (cut it into fine slices by the butcher)

2 cups beef soup

1 1/2 tablespoons pectin powder

A few lovage leaves

3 slices of milk bread

9 oz sauerkraut

4 tablespoons creme fraîche

5 tablespoons sour cream

5 tablespoons sauerkraut juice

1/2 tablespoon tarragon vinegar

1 tablespoon chopped chives

A little horseradish, salt, pepper

1. Bring the soup to a boil with the pectin powder, allow to cool. Allow a little of this to set in the refrigerator. The liquid has to set hard enough to be cut within 1/4 hour, otherwise reheat and add more pectin powder.

2. Finely cut the lovage and dice the milk bread. Mix the lovage, milk bread, sauerkraut, 3 tablespoons crème fraîche and the sour cream, add salt and pepper.

3. Pour enough lukewarm jelly into a terrine mold to cover the bottom well. Allow the jelly to set. Line the bottom and walls of the mold with ox lip.

4. Put in the sauerkraut mixture, cover with ox lip and warm jelly. Allow to cool for at least 1 hour.

5. Cut the terrine into slices and arrange on plates. Also add fine slices of ox lip.

6. Mix 1 tablespoon crème fraîche with sauerkraut juice and tarragon vinegar to make a sauce. Pour this over the terrine and ox lip, sprinkle with chives and horseradish.

Pig's Cheek Salad with Scarlet Runner Beans

Ingredients for 8 servings

8 pigs' cheeks	3 1/2 oz scarlet runner beans
1 onion	1/2 cup to 1 generous cup pumpkin-seed oil
2 teaspoons curing salt	Hot mustard
1 piece of ham rind (optional)	1 crisp-head lettuce
3 cloves of garlic	A little tarragon or balsamic vinegar
1 clove	Horseradish (optional)
1 pimiento	Salt
1 teaspoon unrefined sugar	Pepper

1. Peel and chop the onion. Put the pigs' cheeks into a pan with 2 cups of cold water, curing salt, 2 unpeeled halved cloves of garlic, the clove, pimiento, unrefined sugar and the onion. The cheeks have to be covered with water. Replace the lid and cure for one week in the refrigerator.

2. Boil the cheeks, still in the curing liquid, after adding 2 cups of water and remove the froth formed. Allow the cheeks to simmer for 1 to 1 1/2 hours.

3. To make the bean cream, soak the beans in cold water overnight. Add an unpeeled clove of garlic to this water and, if available, 1 piece of ham rind, and cook the beans until they are tender, about 1 1/2 hours.

4. Drain just enough water from the beans for them to remain covered. Use a hand blender to puree the beans while adding enough pumpkin-seed oil to form a creamy consistency. Add salt, pepper and, if desired, crushed garlic to taste.

5. Put the bean cream onto a plate, lift the cheeks out of the stock, cut them through, lay them on the bean cream and spread a thin film of mustard over them.

6. Wash the lettuce, cut into small pieces and arrange on top of the cheeks. Sprinkle with tarragon or balsamic vinegar and pumpkin-seed oil. Sprinkle with grated horseradish, if desired.

K. and R. Obauer

The salad can be made even more interesting by adding pork hocks. The bean cream is ideal as a sidedish with steamed fish or raw oysters.

Hare Tartlets with Apple and Cabbage Salad

Ingredients for 8 servings (16 tartlets)

7 oz green lentils

9 oz short pastry (see page 78)

Pulses for baking blind

1 lb hare meat (fillets and filleted back)

1 carrot or 2 oz pumpkin

2 to 3 tablespoons peanut oil

1 pinch ground coriander

1 pinch ground ginger (optional)

4 tablespoons milk

4 tablespoons fresh cream

3 egg yolks

1 egg

Salt

Pepper

For the apple and cabbage salad:

14 oz white cabbage

1 dash of cider vinegar

1 apple

Salt

1. Soak the lentils for one hour in water.

2. Preheat the oven to 400 °F. Roll out the pastry. Line the greased soufflé molds with pastry, cover with baking paper and tip in pulses. Bake the pastry blind for about 10 minutes. Remove the baking paper and the pulses.

3. Cut the meat into 1/3 inch cubes. Peel and dice the carrot or pumpkin. Strain the lentils. Sauté the meat, lentils, carrot or pumpkin in peanut oil briefly but do not allow the meat to cook through. Spice with coriander, ginger, salt and pepper.

4. Mix the milk, cream, egg yolks and egg, add salt and pepper. Put the meat mixture into the pastry case and pour the egg mixture over it. Bake the tartlets in the oven for 8 to 10 minutes at 400 °F.

5. To make the salad, wash the white cabbage and chop finely. Add a little salt and mix with a dash of cider vinegar and a grated, unpeeled apple.

6. Remove the tartlets from the molds and serve with apple and cabbage salad.

K. and R. Obauer

These tartlets can be prepared with many different sorts of meat. They taste particularly good when made with venison or stag meat; the best meat to use is from the leg.

Soups

LADLES OF LOVE

Crawfish Soup

Ingredients for 10 servings

40 crawfish

1 tablespoon vinegar

1 teaspoon caraway

3 carrots

2 onions

1/4 stick of celery

2 bulbs of garlic

2 tomatoes

4 tablespoons olive oil

1/2 cup cognac

2 cups fresh cream

2 tablespoons tarragon vinegar

5 coriander seeds

1 teaspoon caraway seeds

5 black peppercorns

1 bay leaf

1/2 sprig of thyme

1 pinch cayenne pepper

A little sea salt

A few tarragon and basil leaves (optional)

2 tablespoons tomato paste

Butter for thickening

A little cornstarch (optional)

Salt

1 handful of fresh herbs (basil, mint or water cress)

1. Lay the crawfish in simmering water with a little vinegar and caraway, cover and boil for one minute. Lift the crawfish out of the water, break out the tails: To do this, twist the head off, break open the first ring of the tail and remove by squeezing out the tail from the end to the front.

2. Coarsely chop the shells. Peel the carrots, onion and celery and cut into pieces; halve the garlic and tomatoes.

3. Heat the olive oil in a casserole and roast the carcasses of the crawfish. As soon as they have gained a little color, add the vegetables and steam. Pour in the cognac, a generous 2 quarts of water, fresh cream and tarragon vinegar. Add the coriander seeds, caraway, peppercorns, bay leaf, thyme, cayenne pepper and sea salt, and fresh tarragon and basil, if desired. Stir in the tomato paste.

4. Simmer the soup for 45 minutes, then strain. Stir in cold butter and possibly a little cornstarch mixed with water to thicken. Beat to a creamy consistency with a hand blender.

5. Put the crawfish meat into soup bowls and pour over the hot soup. Sprinkle with fresh mint, basil or water cress leaves.

K. and R. Obauer

Variation: A lobster soup can be made in the same way. For this, you will need a good 2 lb of lobster (normally 2 lobsters). Do not roast the tomato paste! This is often recommended but can create an unpleasant, bitter flavor. Thyme and caraway should not dominate the taste, use sparingly.

Cold Kohlrabi Soup

Ingredients for 6 to 8 portions

2 kohlrabis

2 shallots

2 eggs

1 generous cup crème fraîche

1 generous cup sour cream

A little lemon juice

1 to 2 teaspoons freshly chopped chervil

(optional)

Salt

Pepper

1. Peel and dice the kohlrabis, peel the shallots and cut into fine slices. Boil the vegetables in 1 1/2 quarts of water until soft, and allow to cool in the liquid.

2. Add the eggs, crème fraîche and sour cream and puree with a hand blender. Pour the soup through a fine sieve to remove the woody parts of the kohlrabi.

3. Season the soup with salt, a little pepper and lemon juice to taste. Sprinkle with chervil, if desired.

K. and R. Obauer

The soup can also be served hot. To do this, mix the crème fraîche, sour cream and 2 tablespoons of butter into the hot vegetable stock and omit the eggs. Smoked or pickled fish is ideal to serve in the soup.

Cream of Parsley Soup

Ingredients for 6 servings

2 turnip-rooted parsley roots

3 shallots

1 tablespoon butter

1 generous cup crème fraîche

1 generous cup fresh cream

2 cups chicken soup

1 egg yolk

1 pinch of grated nutmeg

A little lemon juice

1 tablespoon parsley leaves

Salt

Pepper

1. Peel the parsley roots and cut into slices. Peel and chop the shallots. Sauté the roots and shallots in butter.

2. Pour in the crème fraîche, 3/4 cup of fresh cream, the chicken soup and 1 generous cup water and allow to simmer for 1/4 hour.

3. Puree the soup with a hand blender and thicken by stirring in 1/4 cup of whipped cream and an egg yolk.

4. Season the soup with nutmeg, lemon juice, salt and pepper to taste. Whip with a hand blender and pour through a sieve. Ladle the soup into dishes or bowls and serve sprinkled with parsley.

K. and R. Obauer

The perfect addition to this soup is calf's head (see page 98).

Sorrel Soup

Ingredients for 8 servings

6 shallots

1 clove of garlic

2 tablespoons butter

Generous 4 cups chicken soup

1 generous cup crème fraîche

2 cups sour cream

4 oz sorrel

Juice of 1 lemon

A little cornstarch (optional)

A few sorrel leaves to garnish

Salt · Pepper

1. Peel and chop the shallots and garlic and sauté in butter. Pour in chicken soup and 1 generous cup of water. Stir in the crème fraîche and sour cream and allow to stand for about 1/4 hour.

2. Wash and cut the sorrel. Stir the sorrel, and possibly a little butter, into the soup.

3. Puree the soup with a hand blender and pour through a sieve. If required, thicken by adding a little cornstarch dissolved in water.

4. Season the soup with salt, pepper and lemon juice, serve sprinkled with chopped sorrel leaves.

K. and R. Obauer

Buttered bread sprinkled with chives or sorrel goes well with this soup. The sorrel soup can also be served with fine additions, e.g. poached salmon or salmon trout fillet, fried veal sweetbreads, or raw veal fillet cut into wafer-thin slices.

Bean Soup

Ingredients for 6 servings

3 1/2 oz dried white beans

1 cured pork hock (about 14 oz incl. bones)

2 onions

1 bay leaf

1 clove

3 juniper berries

1 sprig of thyme

3 cloves of garlic

A little mugwort (optional)

1 tablespoon butter

1 generous cup fresh cream

1 dash of olive oil

Salt · Pepper

1. Soak the beans in cold water overnight.

2. Peel 1 onion. Put the cured pork hock in water with the onion, bay leaf, clove, juniper berries, thyme, the unpeeled cloves of garlic and possibly some mugwort. Bring the water to a boil, scoop off the froth. Cover and allow to simmer for approx. 2 1/2 hours (until the bone slips out easily).

3. Lift the hock out of the stock. Dampen a cloth with cold water and use to wrap up the hock (this preserves the fresh color).

4. Peel the second onion, dice and sauté in butter. Pour in 2 cups of the stock and 1 1/2 quarts of water. Drain the beans and add them. Allow the beans to boil for 1 to 1 1/2 hours.

5. Pour the fresh cream and olive oil into the beans, puree and strain.

6. Remove the meat from the bone, chop, heat up in the soup. Season with salt and pepper.

Spring Cream Soup with Ricotta Turnovers

Ingredients for 8 servings

2 small leeks

4 asparagus stalks

2 oz young peas

2 young carrots

5 shallots

5 new potatoes

1 clove of garlic

1 to 2 tablespoons butter

2 cups chicken soup

2 cups fresh cream

11 oz spring herbs (e.g. chervil, wild garlic,

parsley, chives, young spinach, dandelion, sorrel,

ribgrass, arugola, yarrow)

Potato starch (optional)

Grated nutmeg

1 untreated lemon or lime

A few herb leaves to garnish

Salt · Pepper

For the turnovers:

7 oz noodle dough (recipe on page 23)

5 1/2 oz ricotta

1 teaspoon sour cream

1 teaspoon dark breadcrumbs

1 handful of spring herbs (ideally: sorrel, basil,

cress)

Salt · Pepper

1. Peel and wash the leek, asparagus, carrots, shallots, potatoes and garlic and chop into small pieces and shell the peas. Sauté the vegetables in butter, add chicken soup, cream and 4 generous cups of water. Allow to simmer for 1/4 hour.

2. Wash and coarsely chop the herbs and put them into the soup with their stalks. Allow to steep for 1 minute. Puree the soup with the hand blender and strain with a sieve. If required, thicken with a little potato starch. Season the soup with salt, pepper, nutmeg and grated lemon or lime zest.

3. For the turnover filling, chop the herbs, mix the ricotta with sour cream, dark breadcrumbs and herbs. Season with salt and pepper to taste.

4. Roll out the noodle dough, cut into squares and put a spoonful of the ricotta filling in the middle. Fold the pastry into triangles and press the edges down firmly. Lay the turnovers in slightly simmering salted water and cook for two minutes.

5. Serve the ricotta turnovers in the hot soup. Garnish the soup with fresh herbs.

K. and R. Obauer

Instead of adding turnovers to the soup, try steamed fish, mussels or – especially at Easter – wafer-thin slices of kid's liver.

Semolina Soup with Porcini

Ingredients for 4 servings

2 oz bacon
3 shallots
2 oz semolina
3 oz butter
1 1/2 quarts chicken stock
1 pinch grated nutmeg
1 pinch ground caraway
1 clove of garlic
3 small porcini mushrooms (approx. 9 oz)
1 dash of pumpkin-seed oil
Salt
Pepper

1. Dice the bacon, peel and finely chop the shallots.

2. Sauté the semolina, bacon and shallots in 2 oz butter. Pour in the chicken stock and simmer for 1/4 hour. Season the soup with grated nutmeg, a little caraway, salt and pepper.

3. Clean the porcini mushrooms, cut into strips and fry in the remaining butter.

4. Serve the soup in bowls, lay the strips of mushrooms in the soup and season with a dash of pumpkin-seed oil.

Fish Consommé

Ingredients for 8 servings

3 whole Dover sole (approx. 3 1/4 lb)

1/4 fennel

8 shallots

3 1/2 oz mushrooms

1 to 2 tablespoons olive oil

2 cups Riesling wine

1 bay leaf

7 coriander seeds

1 small bulb of garlic

5 peppercorns

2 spring onions

1 handful chanterelles (optional)

1 pinch saffron

1 handful arugola

A little cornstarch (optional)

1 pinch of cayenne pepper (optional)

Sea salt

1. Fillet the sole, pull off the dark skin. Peel the fennel, shallots and mushrooms and cut into fine slices. Wash the fish bones and braise lightly in olive oil with the mushrooms and vegetables.

2. Pour in the wine and 1 1/2 quarts of water and bring to a boil. Add the bay leaf, coriander seeds, the garlic bulb, halved and unpeeled, and the peppercorns. Allow to steep for about 1/2 hour, but no longer boil. Strain.

3. Cut the fish fillets into bite-sized portions, clean the spring onions and the chanterelles and cut into small pieces. Put the fish portions into a pan, add a pinch of saffron, the spring onions and the chanterelles, pour over the hot soup and briefly bring to the boil.

4. Cut the arugola into wide strips and add it to the soup. Slightly thicken the soup by stirring in a little cornstarch. Season with cayenne pepper and sea salt to taste.

K. and R. Obauer

Turbot is also ideal for making a fish consommé. Adding a few scampi can make the soup even more interesting: Shell the scampi prior to boiling them and use the shells like the fish bones. Put the scampi into the soup bowls and cover with the hot soup; they should not be boiled. Finally, perhaps stir in 4 tablespoons of chopped black olives and a little savory.

Jerusalem Artichoke Soup

Ingredients for 8 servings

9 oz Jerusalem artichokes

5 shallots

1 to 2 tablespoons peanut oil

1 generous cup chicken soup

3 1/2 oz mascarpone

1 generous cup fresh cream

Butter for thickening (optional)

Salt

Pepper

1. Wash and brush the artichokes. Peel the shallots and chop with the artichokes. Sauté both in oil.

2. Pour the chicken soup and 2 cups of water into the vegetables and cook the artichokes for about 1/2 hour until tender.

3. Stir in the mascarpone and fresh cream and allow to boil for another 5 minutes.

4. Puree the soup briefly with a hand blender, pour through a sieve, season with salt and pepper. Thicken as required with cold butter.

K. and R. Obauer

Cured, smoked ham can be added in strips, or smoked goose breast. Arugola also goes well in this soup.

Cream of Chestnut Soup

Ingredients for 4 servings

10 chestnuts

2 shallots

1 sprig of rosemary

1/2 cup fresh cream

2 cups chicken stock

1 tablespoon peanut oil

Salt

Pepper

1. Slit the chestnuts and bake in the oven at 430 °F for 10 to 20 minutes until the shells can be removed.

2. Peel the chestnuts and the shallots. Chop the shallots. Slightly roast the chestnuts, shallots and rosemary in peanut oil. Add the cream, chicken stock and water and simmer for 20 minutes.

3. Remove the rosemary from the soup. Puree the soup with a hand blender, pour through a sieve and season with salt and pepper. Add strips of roast pheasant or chicken.

Roast Beef Soup with Butter Quenelles

Ingredients for 4 servings

14 oz roast beef

2 lb (approx.) beef chine

4 1/2 lb red beef bones

2 onions

4 carrots

2 turnip-rooted parsley roots

1/4 celeriac

A few lovage leaves

10 peppercorns

1 bay leaf

5 coriander seeds

1 to 2 tablespoons chopped chives

For the butter quenelles:

4 eggs

3 1/2 oz butter

7 oz flour

Salt

1. Chop the bones into small pieces, put into almost boiling water and allow to boil briefly. Pour off the water. Put the bones into cold water again, bring to a boil and scoop off the froth.

2. Wash the chine in cold water. Peel and wash the vegetables and cut into small pieces. Add the chine, vegetables and spices to the steeping bones. Allow to simmer for about 5 hours.

3. For the butter quenelles: Separate the egg yolks from the whites. Beat the butter with the yolks and a little salt and work in the flour. Whisk the egg whites with a pinch of salt until stiff and fold into the yolk mixture.

4. Use a tablespoon to scoop out a little from the mixture and form an oval ball with the palms of your hands. Put the quenelles into simmering water, replace lid and allow to steep for about 10 minutes. Lift out of the water and rinse in cold water.

5. Cut the roast beef into as thin slices as possible. Put the quenelles into the soup bowls, cover with raw roast beef slices and pour over the strained soup.

6. Cut the chine into slices and also add to the soup. Sprinkle with chives and serve.

K. and R. Obauer

This soup also tastes wonderful cold: Stir the cold soup with a whisk to dissolve the jelly, ladle into dishes and put in the cold quenelles and wafer-thin slices of meat. A few dashes of balsamic vinegar and freshly grated Parmesan cheese make the soup even more refreshing.

Potato Consommé

Ingredients for 4 servings

2 half-cooked potatoes

8 young carrots

4 shallots

2 oz bacon

1 bay leaf

1 teaspoon dried marjoram

1 dash of wine vinegar

1 teaspoon caraway

1 teaspoon cornflour

1 to 2 tablespoons freshly chopped herbs

(parsley, lovage and savory)

Salt

Pepper

1. Peel and dice the potatoes. Peel the carrots and slice finely, peel the shallots and chop finely.

2. Boil the vegetables with 4 generous cups of water and simmer for 5 to 8 minutes.

3. Dice the bacon. Add the bacon, bay leaf, marjoram, vinegar and caraway to the soup.

4. Mix the cornflour with 1 tablespoon water and slightly thicken the soup. Season the soup with salt and pepper and serve sprinkled with fresh herbs.

Salsify Soup with Saffron

Ingredients for 6 servings

4 salsify roots (approx. 5 1/2 oz)

2 shallots

1/2 garlic clove

2 tablespoons butter

1 1/2 cups chicken soup

1 generous cup fresh cream

1 tablespoon crème fraîche

1 sachet saffron

Salt

Pepper

1. Wash the salsify, peel and cut into fine slices. Peel shallots and garlic and cut into fine slices.

2. Sauté the vegetables in butter, add the chicken soup and not quite a cup of water. Stir in the cream and crème fraîche and simmer for 1/4 hour.

3. Puree the soup with a hand blender, pour through a sieve, stir in the saffron, salt and pepper. Allow the soup to stand for another 10 minutes.

K. and R. Obauer

You can also make this soup with beef. The best way is: Simmer 1 lb shin of beef in 4 generous cups of water with the usual spices and vegetables for 3 to 4 hours on a very low heat. Continue as above. Instead of chicken soup, use the stock from the shin of beef. Lay pieces of shin in the soup to serve.

Fish

FRESH FROM THE LAKE, RIVER AND SEA

Trout Strudel

Ingredients for 6 servings

2 trout, 12 oz each

1 generous cup fresh cream

1 egg

Juice of 1 lemon

7 oz mushrooms

4 1/2 oz crème fraîche

9 oz strudel pastry

A little butter for brushing

2 shallots

1 tomato

A generous 1/2 cup fish stock

1/2 cup white wine

4 tablespoons dry vermouth (e.g. Noilly Prat)

Salt

Pepper

1. Fillet the trout. Cut the fillets from one trout into small pieces. Cut each of the other two fillets from the second trout into three pieces.

2. Grind the small pieces of trout with half the cream, the egg, lemon juice, salt and pepper in the blender (all ingredients must be well chilled).

3. Clean the mushrooms and chop finely. Boil 5 1/2 oz of mushrooms with the crème fraîche to form a thickish cream. Season with salt, pepper and a squeeze of lemon juice.

4. Cut the strudel dough into six squares measuring 5 x 5 inches. Lay one strudel leaf into a lightly buttered coffee cup, press in well with the fingertips, allow the edges to fall outside the cup. Put in a layer of filling, add a layer of mushroom puree and a piece of trout fillet. Finish with filling and mushroom puree. Butter the overhanging edges of the strudel dough and close over the filling.

5. Preheat the oven to 430 °F. Slide the trout strudel out of the cups onto a greased baking tray, the closed ends should be upwards. Bake in the preheated oven for 12 minutes.

6. For the sauce: Peel and chop the shallots, dip the tomato into boiling water, skin, remove the flesh and chop finely. Bring the remaining cream with the fish stock, white wine, vermouth, shallots, tomato and remaining chopped mushrooms to the boil. Boil until the liquid is reduced to half.

7. Pour the sauce through a sieve. Stir in enough butter to make the sauce very creamy. Season with salt, pepper and a dash of lemon juice to taste.

8. Serve the trout strudel with the sauce.

Pancake with Smoked Trout and Sauerkraut

Ingredients for 4 servings

For the pancake mix:

6 eggs

6 tablespoons fresh cream

1 pinch of cayenne pepper · Salt

Oil for frying

For the filling:

1 smoked trout

5 1/2 oz crème fraîche

4 tablespoons sour cream

7 oz sauerkraut

For the sauce:

Trout skin and bones

1/2 bay leaf

2 peppercorns

1 small clove of garlic

3 1/2 oz butter

1 teaspoon chopped fennel green or dill

A little lemon juice

Salt

Pepper

1. For the filling: Fillet the smoked trout, remove the bones and skin. Pull out any fine bones remaining with tweezers. Keep the bones and skin for preparing the sauce. Cut the trout flesh into small pieces, mash with a fork and mix with crème fraîche and sour cream.

2. For the sauce: Put the trout bones and skin into a pan with the bay leaf, peppercorns and the peeled clove of garlic. Pour over 1 generous cup water (just to cover them) and bring to a boil. Allow to steep on a very low heat for about 1/2 hour.

3. For the pancake: Beat the eggs with the cream, season with salt and cayenne pepper. Fry small pancakes in a frying pan in very little oil.

4. Lay the pancakes on the work surface beside each other, spread the trout filling and sauerkraut on them so that the sauerkraut peeps out at the edges after rolling them up.

5. Pour the stock for the sauce through a fine sieve and bring to a boil. Remove from heat, add the chilled butter in small pieces and beat the sauce with the hand blender. Season with fennel green, lemon juice, salt and pepper.

6. Serve the trout pancakes with the sauce. If the pancakes have cooled while the sauce is being made, lay them on a buttered baking tray and briefly warm them in the oven.

K. and R. Obauer

The sauce tastes particularly nice if dried porcini are added before boiling.

Char with Kohlrabi and Lime Sauce

Ingredients for 4 servings

8 char fillets
2 kohlrabis
2 tablespoons butter
2 tablespoons crème fraîche
3 limes
Cress for garnishing (optional)
Salt
Pepper

1. Peel the kohlrabis and cut into segments or dice. Put into a pan and add a little salt, pepper, 1 tablespoon of butter and enough water to cover the vegetables. Simmer for about 10 to 15 minutes.

2. Halve the char fillets. As soon as the kohlrabi is almost tender, lay the char on top, cover and steam for about 3 minutes.

3. Lift the kohlrabi and fish out of the stock and arrange on warm plates. Mix 1 generous cup of stock with crème fraîche, 1 tablespoon of butter and the juice of the limes. Season the sauce with salt and pepper, pour the sauce over the fish. Sprinkle with lime zest and, if desired, cress. Serve potato dumplings to accompany the fish.

Whitefish with Sauerkraut and Anchovy Sauce

Ingredients for 4 servings

8 whitefish fillets, boneless

14 oz small potatoes

1 carrot

2 oz celeriac

1 parsnip

3 shallots

4 tablespoons white wine

1 pinch sugar

14 oz sauerkraut

1/2 cup chicken stock

1/2 cup fresh cream

2 tablespoons crème fraîche

1 tablespoon anchovy paste

Butter to thicken the sauce

Juice of 1 lemon

Salt

Pepper

1. Boil the potatoes in their skins, peel them.

2. Peel the carrot, celeriac, parsnip and shallots, dice and boil for about 15 minutes in the wine and a pinch of sugar.

3. Mix the sauerkraut with the boiled vegetables and stock and heat.

4. For the sauce: Boil the chicken stock with the fresh cream, crème fraîche and anchovy paste and beat until creamy. Add enough butter for the sauce to take on a creamy consistency. Season with salt, pepper and lemon juice.

5. Lay the fish fillets on the sauerkraut, cover with the anchovy sauce and add the potatoes. Cover and steam the whitefish and potatoes for 5 minutes.

6. Arrange the sauerkraut, potatoes and fish fillets on four plates. Briefly mix the sauce again in the blender and sprinkle over the fish and sauerkraut.

K. and R. Obauer

Instead of chicken stock, you could use beef soup.
If you would like a richer flavor,
the fish can be fried instead of steamed.

Eel with Dark Breadcrumbs and Smoked Fish Sauce

Ingredients for 4 servings

30 scarlet runner beans

1 piece of ham rind

Dried thyme

2 eels, each a good 1 1/2 lb

Juice of 1 lemon

2 tablespoons dark breadcrumbs

2 shallots

9 oz bones and skin from smoked fish

(e. g. from trout or salmon)

1 small bay leaf

2 oz dried porcini mushrooms

Butter to thicken the sauce

8 cloves of garlic

Olive oil for frying

2 slices of ham (from the leg)

1 dash of vinegar

Salt

Pepper

1. Soak the beans in water overnight, strain and boil until tender in 1 1/2 quarts of water with the ham rind and a little thyme for about 1 hour. Strain the beans.

2. Fillet the eels, score the skin at intervals of just under an inch and cut the fillets into three pieces. Sprinkle with lemon juice and season with salt and pepper. Press the skinless side into dark breadcrumbs.

3. For the sauce: Peel the shallots and cut into fine slices. Slowly bring the skin and bones of the smoked fish to the boil in 2 cups water. Remove the froth. Add shallots, bay leaf and porcini. Simmer the stock until the liquid has reduced by half.

4. Strain the stock and season with salt and pepper. Mix in enough cold butter to produce a slightly creamy sauce.

5. Preheat the oven to 430 °F. Simmer the unpeeled garlic cloves in olive oil for 10 minutes, remove from the fat and peel.

6. Put a little olive oil in an ovenproof dish, lay the eel fillets inside with the skin face down and bake in the preheated oven for about 7 minutes.

7. Dice the ham. Mix the beans with the ham, deep-fried garlic, a dash of olive oil and vinegar. Season with salt and pepper. Serve the eel with the sauce and beans.

Eel with Spiced Rice

Ingredients for 4 servings

14 oz eel

2 cups long-grained rice

1 tablespoon butter

2 spring onions

2 shallots

2 cloves of garlic

1/2 carrot

1 small piece fresh ginger

5 tablespoons peanut oil

1/2 teaspoon paprika (mild)

1/2 teaspoon curry powder

1 tablespoon soy sauce

1 pinch of cayenne pepper

Zest of an untreated lemon

Salt

Pepper

1. Fry the rice briefly in the butter. Add 4 cups of water and steam the rice until tender. Strain and rinse with cold water.

2. Fillet the eel, but do not skin it, and cut into 3/4 inch pieces. Peel the spring onions and cut into 2 1/2 inches pieces, peel the shallots and garlic and dice finely; peel the carrot and cut into julienne pieces, clean the ginger and dice finely.

3. Heat 1 tablespoon peanut oil (preferably in an iron pan) and fry the pieces of eel for a few minutes.

4. Add the vegetables, ginger and paprika, curry powder, 4 tablespoons of peanut oil, soy sauce and cayenne pepper. Fry everything for a few minutes.

5. Add the rice and continue to fry until the rice has browned a little.

6. Serve in soup dishes and sprinkle with grated lemon zest. Add salt if necessary.

K. and R. Obauer

*This dish resembles "Mongolian Firepot".
It also tastes excellent with octopus,
scampi and other fish or seafood with firm
flesh and with chicken.*

Pike Perch with Anchovies and Bean Salad

Ingredients for 4 servings

4 pike perch fillets, together about 1 1/4 lb

9 oz white or scarlet runner beans

1 bay leaf

1 sprig of rosemary

2 sprigs of savory

A piece of ham rind (optional)

1 onion

2 oz anchovy fillets

4 beef tomatoes

1 generous dash of white wine vinegar

1 teaspoon sugar

1 teaspoon crushed black pepper

4 to 5 tablespoons olive oil

1 chili, cut into very fine strips

1 tablespoon chopped chervil, tarragon and lovage

2 to 3 tablespoons butter

Juice of 1 lemon

1 to 2 teaspoons soy sauce

A little anchovy paste

1 bunch of parsley

White breadcrumbs for coating

3 tablespoons clarified butter

Salt · Pepper

1. Soak the beans overnight. Strain, put into a pan with enough fresh, cold water to cover. Add bay leaf, rosemary, savory and, if desired, a piece of ham rind. Boil the beans for approx. 1 1/2 hours until tender. Pour off the water from the beans, saving only a small quantity.

2. Peel and chop the onion. Mix the anchovy fillets with the beans and onions.

3. Core the tomatoes, lay them briefly in boiling water, rinse with cold water, skin and remove the flesh. Dice the flesh and add to the beans. Stir in the white wine vinegar, sugar, crushed black pepper, a generous amount of olive oil, the chili and the chopped herbs.

4. Melt the butter. Salt the pike perch fillets, sprinkle with lemon juice and a little soy sauce and spread with a little anchovy paste. Wash the parsley, dab dry and chop finely. Toss the pike perch fillets in the parsley, dip them in the melted butter and press into the white breadcrumbs.

5. Fry the pike perch fillets in clarified butter on a low heat with the skin side down. Turn after 3 to 4 minutes (total cooking time 6 to 8 minutes).

6. Serve the pike perch fillets with the bean salad (the salad tastes best while it is lukewarm).

K. and R. Obauer

The bean salad should taste a little hot.
Cayenne pepper can be used instead of the chili.

Pike Perch with Balsamic Vinegar, Jerusalem Artichoke and Shallots

Ingredients for 4 servings

12 shallots

14 oz Jerusalem artichokes

2 tablespoons peanut oil

1 tablespoon clarified butter

1 sprig of fresh thyme

1 1/4 lb pike perch fillet

Flour for coating

2 tablespoons olive oil

2 tablespoons balsamic vinegar

2 tablespoons brown chicken stock (optional)

Sea salt

A few sprigs of parsley for deep-frying

Salt

Pepper

1. Preheat the oven to 390 °F.

2. Peel the shallots, wash and brush the artichokes and cut into pieces as big as the shallots. Put the artichokes and shallots into an ovenproof dish with the peanut oil, clarified butter and thyme and braise for 20 minutes (the artichokes have to be soft). Remove from the oven.

3. Cut each fish fillet into 8 pieces, season with salt and pepper and toss in the flour. Heat a little olive oil in a pan. Lay the fillets skin down in the pan, place the pan into the preheated oven and bake the pike perch for about 5 minutes.

4. Lift the vegetables out of the ovenproof dish. Stir in balsamic vinegar to dissolve the residue and add brown chicken stock if available.

5. Distribute the vegetables on 4 plates, lay the fish on top and sprinkle with the juice from the vegetables. Grind fresh black pepper and sea salt over the plates. Garnish with deep-fried parsley if desired.

K. and R. Obauer

As far as clarified butter goes: This fat is ideal for frying and baking. It has the full aroma of butter, but is far more heat-resistant. Clarified butter can also be stored longer than butter. It should have a permanent place in the refrigerator!

Catfish Roast

Ingredients for 4 servings

14 oz catfish fillet

1 1/4 lb potatoes, half-cooked

Olive oil for frying

2 cloves of garlic

2 tablespoons balsamic vinegar

1 tablespoon chives, chopped

1 tablespoon lovage, cut in strips

For the sauce:

1 tablespoon black olives, chopped

1 tablespoon salted capers

1 teaspoon rosemary, chopped

Juice of 2 lemons

Salt · pepper

10 tablespoons olive oil

1/2 clove of garlic, crushed

1. Wash the potatoes and boil them in salted water. Peel and cut into slices. Fry the potatoes in olive oil until crispy and season with salt.

2. Peel the garlic and cut into slices. Cut the catfish fillet into pieces just over an inch wide and fry in olive oil in a pan with the skin side down. Just before they are done (8 minutes) add the slices of garlic.

3. Arrange the potatoes and catfish on 4 plates, sprinkle with chives and lovage, cover with the sauce that is mixed together cold and sprinkle with balsamic vinegar.

K. and R. Obauer

This dish also tastes particularly good with fresh wild garlic.

Steamed Tench with Paprika and White Cabbage

Ingredients for 4 servings

Fillets from 4 tench, approx. 1 1/4 lb

2 onions

1 clove of garlic

1 tablespoon butter

1 teaspoon sugar

Just over 3 cups beef soup

4 tablespoons mild paprika

2 beef tomatoes

1/2 bay leaf

1 pinch of cayenne pepper

1/4 head of white cabbage

4 tablespoons sour cream

Salt

1. Peel the onions and garlic, cut into fine slices and sauté in butter. Stir in the sugar, pour on the beef stock or water and stir in the paprika.

2. Slit the tomatoes in a cross, drop briefly in hot water, rinse with cold water and skin. Remove the seeds from the tomatoes and chop the flesh. Add the tomato flesh, the bay leaf, cayenne pepper and salt to the soup. Boil until the liquid is reduced to about two-thirds.

3. Remove the stalk from the cabbage and cut it into fine slices (strips about 3/4 inch long). Put the cabbage into the soup, cover and simmer for about 3 minutes.

4. Skin the tench fillets, remove any bones. Lay the fillets on the cabbage, add a little salt and steam for about 5 minutes on the cabbage.

5. Arrange the cabbage on four plates, lay the fish fillets on top and add 1 tablespoon sour cream.

K. and R. Obauer

This method of preparation is suitable for all kinds of freshwater fish with a high fat content, e.g. eel, carp or catfish. The ideal accompaniment is spaetzle or potatoes steamed in their skins. Add wild garlic in spring!

Pike Rolls with Bacon and Kidney Beans

Ingredients for 4 servings

1 1/2 lb pike fillet

2 oz bacon

Several small bay leaves

4 1/2 lb broad beans in pods

1 generous cup fresh cream

1 teaspoon finely chopped rosemary

Butter for thickening the sauce

1 finely chopped clove of garlic

1 to 2 tablespoons olive oil for frying

Salt

Pepper

1. Cut the bones out of the pike fillet with a sharp, narrow knife and divide the fillet into pieces just over an inch wide. Roll the pike up into coils, cover with a bay leaf and a piece of bacon and tie up with kitchen thread.

2. Shell the beans, blanche briefly, rinse with iced water and peel.

3. Allow the fresh cream to slowly simmer with the rosemary. Add 4 tablespoons of the water from the beans and mix in enough butter to give the sauce a delicate creamy consistency. Season with salt pepper and garlic.

4. Fry the pike rolls in olive oil for about 5 minutes on each side.

5. Warm the beans in the sauce. Remove the thread from the pike rolls. Serve the pike rolls with the beans and the sauce.

Carp in Vinegar Sauce

Ingredients for 4 servings

4 fillets from a leather carp

1/2 to 1 tablespoon aniseed

3 sprigs of basil

3 shallots

1 tablespoon vinegar

1 bunch of chives

Salt

For the vegetable stock:

5 small carrots

8 shallots

1 small bunch of thyme

1/2 cup vinegar (5 % acid)

3 1/2 oz sugar

For the sauce:

4 shallots

1 clove of garlic

1 generous cup vegetable stock

1/2 cup white wine

1 tablespoon crème fraîche

Butter for thickening

1 pinch of ground turmeric

Salt

Pepper

1. Lay the carp fillets on a board with the skin side up and make deep cuts at intervals of just over an inch (do not cut right through). Cut the carp fillets scored in this way into portions.

2. Heat a good 3 cups of water with salt, a little aniseed, basil sprigs, peeled shallots and vinegar in a pot and steam the fillets over the liquid. Wash the chives and chop.

3. For the stock: Peel the carrots and shallots and cut into fine slices. Bring to a boil with 4 generous cups of water. Add the sprigs of thyme, vinegar and sugar and simmer for 2 minutes. Strain through a fine sieve.

4. For the sauce: Peel the shallots and garlic and cut into fine slices. Boil in 1 generous cup of stock and the white wine until the liquid has reduced by half. Thicken the sauce by stirring in cold butter and a little crème fraîche and season with salt and pepper (if desired, stir in a little turmeric).

5. Serve the carp with the sauce and lots of chives.

K. and R. Obauer

Boiled potatoes or noodles go well with this. The sauce for this dish only uses a quarter of the vegetable stock. The rest can be put into airtight jars (with the vegetables) and stored for a long time.

Sea Bass with Daikon Radish and Spiced Butter Sauce

Ingredients for 4 servings

4 sea bass, each between 9 oz and 11 oz, scaled

1 1/4 lb daikon radish

1 1/2 tablespoons sugar

4 tablespoons tarragon vinegar

2 shallots

1/2 carrot

1 generous cup white wine

1/2 clove of garlic

1/2 teaspoon curry powder

1 tablespoon crème fraîche

Butter to thicken the sauce

1 pinch cayenne pepper

A few chopped wild garlic leaves (optional)

Salt

Pepper

1. Peel the radish and grate it into a small pan. Pour in enough water to just cover the radish. Add 1 tablespoon sugar and simmer for 5 minutes. Add a dash of tarragon vinegar, season with salt and pepper and mix.

2. Peel the shallots and the carrot half and cut into fine slices. Boil with the remaining vinegar, white wine, 1 generous cup water, remaining sugar and the crushed garlic clove until the liquid has reduced to half.

3. Strain the stock, stir in curry powder and crème fraîche. Whisk in enough cold butter to make the sauce creamy. Season with salt, pepper and cayenne pepper.

4. Score the fish four times on both sides, salt and steam for 10 minutes.

5. Arrange the radish on four plates. Lay the fish on top and serve with the sauce. Sprinkle with wild garlic if desired.

K. and R. Obauer

*Whitefish or salmon are also a
treat prepared in this way.
The best accompaniment to this dish
is fluffy mashed potatoes.*

Sole with Green Beans, Peaches and Scampi

Ingredients for 4 servings

12 sole fillets with skin, about 1 1/4 lb total

8 scampi

12 oz haricot and/or runner beans

1 young kohlrabi

1 small piece of fresh ginger

1 untreated lemon

1 ripe peach with firm flesh

4 spring onions

2 tablespoons olive oil

2 tablespoons soy sauce

2 tablespoons fish or chicken stock

Butter

Salt

For the sauce:

1 clove of garlic

6 coriander seeds

2 tablespoons lemon juice

4 tablespoons peanut oil

1 tablespoon soy sauce

1 pinch of sugar

1. For the sauce: peel the garlic and dice finely. Crush the coriander seeds with a pestle and mortar. Mix all ingredients together well.

2. Clean the haricots and beans, peel the kohlrabi and cut into segments. Blanche the haricots, beans and kohlrabi, strain and rinse in cold water.

3. Chop the ginger into small pieces (about 1 teaspoon), grate off the lemon zest. Cut the peach into segments. Prepare the spring onions and cut into 1 1/4 inches pieces.

4. Heat the olive oil in a pan and quickly sauté the haricots, beans, kohlrabi, spring onions, ginger and lemon zest. Pour in soy sauce and fish or chicken stock. Add the peach and toss.

5. Salt and steam the sole fillets (if you do not have a steamer, lay the sole fillets in a lightly buttered pan, add a little water, cover and cook).

6. Shell the scampi but leave the tail on. Fry in very hot olive oil for about 1/2 minute. Remove from the pan and sprinkle with lemon juice.

7. Arrange the sole fillets and scampi on the vegetables, pour over sauce and serve.

Without Meat

CABBAGE, ROOTS AND OTHER VEGETABLES

Cheese Custard with Root Milk

Ingredients for 8 to 10 servings

4 oz mild hard cheese or Fontina cheese

1 clove of garlic

1 generous cup milk

1 generous cup fresh cream

4 egg yolks

4 eggs

1 pinch of nutmeg

Salt

Pepper

Butter for the mold

For the sauce:

2 oz carrots

1/2 oz celeriac

2 oz turnip-rooted parsley

1/2 oz Jerusalem artichokes

1 onion

1 generous cup milk

1 generous cup fresh cream

Salt

Pepper

1. Preheat the oven to 340 °F.

2. Grate or chop the cheese. Peel and crush the garlic. Whisk all ingredients for the custard over steam until the cheese has melted (no longer).

3. Grease a terrine mold or ovenproof dish with the butter. Pour in the liquid and place the mold in a larger dish of water. Bake in the preheated oven for 35 to 40 minutes. Test with a needle: Insert a thick needle into the custard and leave for a few seconds, remove, and if the needle is lukewarm where it has been pushed into the custard, the custard is ready. Feel the needle with your lips!

4. Prepare the vegetables for the sauce and chop. Simmer the vegetables with the milk and cream for 15 minutes. Season with salt and pepper, puree with a hand blender and press through a fine sieve. If the sauce is too thick, add a little milk.

5. Scoop small ovals out of the custard with a spoon. Pour the root sauce over them.

K. and R. Obauer

*Fried chanterelles,
porcini or white truffles go well with this.*

Creamed Mushrooms

Ingredients for 4 servings

2 lb mushrooms

4 shallots or 1 small onion

1 clove of garlic

1 tablespoon butter

7 oz crème fraîche

Cornstarch (optional)

1 to 2 tablespoons finely chopped herbs

(lovage, parsley, chives, fennel green)

1 pinch of caraway

Salt

Pepper

1. Prepare the mushrooms. Finely chop the shallots or onion and garlic and sauté in butter. Add the mushrooms, salt and pepper, cover and steam for 5 minutes.

2. Strain the juice from frying and mix it with crème fraîche. If necessary, mix in a little cornstarch to thicken.

3. Add the caraway and herbs and bring the mushrooms to a boil again.

4. Serve the mushrooms with butter quenelles (see page 47) or potato dumplings.

Baked Parasols with Mushroom Sauce

Ingredients for 4 servings

4 medium or 8 small parasol mushrooms

2 eggs, flour and breadcrumbs for coating

Vegetable oil for frying

Salt

For the sauce:

7 oz mushrooms

4 shallots

2 cloves of garlic

1 tablespoon oil

1 tablespoon freshly chopped seasonal herbs

(e.g. parsley, chervil, chives)

1 teaspoon white peppercorns

1 generous cup sour cream

1 teaspoon sugar

1 tablespoon sherry or balsamic vinegar

1 pinch of cayenne pepper

Salt

1. Cut off the stems of the parasol mushrooms. Beat the eggs in a dish, put the flour and breadcrumbs each into a dish. Dip the caps of the mushrooms first in the flour, then in the eggs and finally in the breadcrumbs and fry in a pan in hot vegetable oil.

2. For the sauce: Prepare the mushrooms, shallots and garlic and chop into small pieces. Fry in oil until the water forming has evaporated.

3. Mix the herbs, crushed peppercorns, sour cream, sugar, vinegar, cayenne pepper and a little salt together.

4. Season the fried parasol mushrooms with salt and pepper and serve with the sauce.

Wild Garlic and Cream Cheese Flan with Pine Nuts

Ingredients for two flans 10 inches in diameter

For the pastry lining:

7 oz finely ground flour

4 oz cold butter

1 egg

1 to 2 tablespoons cold water

Salt

For the filling:

5 1/2 oz spinach

30 wild garlic leaves

10 basil leaves

3 tablespoons pine nuts

2 eggs

5 tablespoons grated Parmesan cheese

4 tablespoons olive oil

3 1/2 oz cream cheese (goats' cheese or ricotta are best)

For the sauce:

2 eggs

4 tablespoons olive oil

1 tablespoon lemon juice

Salt

Pepper

1. Crumble the cold butter into the flour, knead quickly with the egg, water and a little salt. Wrap in transparent foil and leave to stand in a cold place for about 1/2 hour.

2. Preheat the oven to 430 °F. Roll out the pastry to about 1/10 inch and line a dish with the pastry so that it hangs over the edge (the pastry will shrink in the oven). Line with greaseproof paper and fill with dried beans or other pulses and prebake the pastry in the oven for 15 minutes. Remove the paper and pulses (these can be used for years for baking blind).

3. For the filling: Wash, clean and coarsely chop the spinach and wild garlic. Crush in a mortar with the basil, pine nuts, eggs, Parmesan cheese and olive oil for about 1 minute. Fill the prepared pastry case with the mixture, cover with cream cheese and bake for 15 minutes at 390 °F.

4. For the sauce: Hard boil the eggs, peel and finely chop them. Mix with olive oil, lemon juice, salt and pepper.

5. Allow the cake to cool a little before serving, preferably warm, with the sauce.

K. and R. Obauer

This flan is an ideal accompaniment for smoked fish. The pastry will turn out better if large quantities are made. The ingredients given here are enough for two flans. The remaining dough can be kept wrapped in transparent foil in the refrigerator for up to one week without it losing in quality.

Asparagus with Morels, Nettle and New Potatoes

Ingredients for 4 servings

11 oz small new potatoes

2 lb thick asparagus

1 teaspoon sugar

11 oz fresh morels

2 shallots

1/2 cup fresh cream

4 tablespoons cognac

A piece of ham rind (optional)

Butter for thickening the sauce

A little cornstarch (optional)

2 oz small nettle leaves

Salt

1. Thoroughly wash the potatoes and boil in their skins in salted water until tender.

2. Wash the asparagus, peel and cut off the woody ends. Boil the asparagus in water with sugar and salt until cooked but firm. Rinse in iced water.

3. Wash the morels well in ice-cold water. Cut off the stems. Peel the shallots and cut into fine slices. Gently simmer the morel stems and shallots in a mixture of 1/2 cup water, the cream and cognac until the liquid has reduced by half; if desired, also add a piece of ham rind.

4. Strain the liquid and whisk in enough cold butter to make a sauce with a creamy consistency (possibly thicken with a little cornstarch dissolved in water).

5. Wash the nettle leaves. Slightly brown 2 tablespoons of butter in a casserole and toss the nettle leaves in this briefly.

6. Cover and fry the morels in 2 tablespoons butter (even better: 1 tablespoon butter and 2 tablespoons peanut oil).

7. Arrange the asparagus and morels in soup dishes and cover with the sauce. Put the nettles on top. Serve with the unpeeled potatoes.

K. and R. Obauer

Instead of these potatoes, mashed potatoes can also be served sprinkled with cress or sorrel.

Asparagus Towers with Parmesan Sauce

Ingredients for 4 main courses
(or 8 appetizers)

11 oz asparagus

1 shallot

1 generous cup fresh cream

1 tablespoon butter

2 tablespoons flour

1/2 cup milk

1/2 oz grated Parmesan cheese

1 egg

4 egg yolks

Butter and breadcrumbs for the molds

A few basil leaves

Salt

For the sauce:

1/2 cup milk

1/2 cup fresh cream

4 tablespoons grated Parmesan cheese

2 tablespoons buttermilk curd or low-fat curd

1/2 clove of garlic

1 pinch of ground caraway

Salt

Pepper

1. Peel the asparagus and cut off the woody ends. Cut the peeled asparagus (about 7 oz) into thin slices. Peel and chop the shallot.

2. Simmer the shallot and asparagus in the cream with a little salt until the liquid has reduced by half. Puree with a hand blender.

3. Heat the butter, stir in the flour and steam. Pour in the milk while continually stirring. Add the grated Parmesan cheese and cook until a creamy mass forms.

4. Allow to cool. Whisk in the egg and egg yolks. Mix this béchamel sauce with the asparagus puree.

5. Brush eight molds with melted butter and line with breadcrumbs. Lay basil leaves in the bottom and pour in the mixture. Put the molds in the top of a steamer and cook for 15 to 20 minutes (or poach in the oven standing in a vessel of water at 350 °F).

6. For the sauce: Boil the milk and cream, whisk in the Parmesan cheese and buttermilk or low-fat curds. Season with crushed garlic, caraway, salt and pepper. Mix to produce a creamy sauce.

7. Turn the asparagus towers out onto plates and surround with the sauce.

K. and R. Obauer

This dish is ideal for using up asparagus without tips. The fine tips can be used to accompany fish or meat dishes.
If the asparagus is cut into fine slices before cooking, the mass does not have to be passed through a sieve.

Salsify Gratin

Ingredients for 4 servings

6 tablespoons green lentils	
8 pieces of salsify	
Butter for the mold	
2 oz chanterelle or shiitake mushrooms	
3 1/2 oz spicy hard cheese	
1 generous cup fresh cream	
1/2 cup milk	
Salt	
Pepper	

1. Soak the lentils in cold water for 1 hour.

2. Wash the salsify in iced water, peel and cut to fit in the pan. Boil for about 20 minutes in salted water until they are soft.

3. Brush a gratin mold with plenty of butter. Cut the salsify into 2 inches lengths and put into the mold with the lentils.

4. Clean the mushrooms, cut into fine slices and spread on the salsify. Preheat the oven to 390 °F.

5. Grate the cheese, mix the cream, milk and cheese together, add a moderate amount of salt and pepper (the hard cheese is spicy enough). Pour this mixture into the mold and bake in the oven for 15 to 20 minutes.

Swiss Chard Roulade with Rice and Saffron

Ingredients for 4 servings

2 shallots

4 1/2 oz long-grained rice

1 to 2 tablespoons butter

1/2 cup chicken stock or soup

1 pinch of saffron

1/2 red bell pepper

6 okra pods (optional)

1 tablespoon curds

3 tablespoons sour cream

4 tablespoons olive oil

1 pinch of cayenne pepper

1 pinch of cumin

1 dash of soy sauce

12 Swiss chard leaves

Butter for the dish

A little balsamic or rice vinegar

Salt

1. Peel and chop the shallots. Sauté in butter with the rice, add the chicken stock and 1/2 cup water. Add the salt, saffron, red pepper and, if available, the okra pods. Steam the rice until soft.

2. Take the vegetables out of the rice and chop into small pieces. Mix the curds with sour cream, vegetables and a little olive oil, season with cayenne pepper, cumin and soy sauce. Mix this with the rice.

3. Preheat the oven to 390 °F. Wash the Swiss chard leaves and dab them dry. Fill with the rice mixture, roll up and turn in the ends to prevent the filling from coming out.

4. Put the roulades in a buttered dish, brush with a little melted butter and heat in the oven for about 10 minutes.

5. If desired, sprinkle the roulades with a little balsamic or rice vinegar before serving.

K. and R. Obauer

This roulade tastes excellent with steamed fish. It can also be coated in breadcrumbs like Wiener Schnitzel and served with heavier dishes (roasted liver, for example) or as a main course.

Stuffed Kohlrabi

Ingredients for 4 servings

1 egg

4 kohlrabis

3 1/2 oz chanterelles

2 shallots

1 tablespoon butter

1 thick slice of white bread

1/2 cup sour cream

1 pinch of ground coriander

1 pinch of caraway

A little freshly chopped chervil

3 to 4 tablespoons olive oil

1 to 2 teaspoons lemon juice

Salt

1. Boil the egg until hard and peel it.

2. Cut the cap with the leaves from the kohlrabi. Peel and hollow out the lower part so that the sides are not quite half an inch thick. Chop the flesh removed.

3. Clean the chanterelles, peel the shallots and chop into small pieces. Sauté in butter.

4. Cut the crust from the white bread and mix with the kohlrabi flesh, chanterelles and 3 tablespoons sour cream. Grate the egg and stir in. Season the mixture with coriander, caraway, chervil and salt and stuff the kohlrabi.

5. Preheat the oven to 390 °F. Replace the kohlrabi caps and tie up with kitchen thread so the kohlrabi leaves fold around the kohlrabi.

6. Put not too little olive oil, a few tablespoons of water and the remaining sour cream into an ovenproof dish and mix. Place the kohlrabi in the dish and bake in the oven for about 45 minutes.

7. Remove the thread before serving, arrange the kohlrabi on plates and sprinkle a little lemon juice over them. Serve with the sauce.

Zucchini Noodles

Ingredients for 4 servings

1 lb small zucchini

1 onion or 5 shallots

2 cloves of garlic

4 to 5 tablespoons olive oil

1 sprig of savory

1/2 cup sour cream

14 oz noodles

1 to 2 tablespoons pumpkin-seed oil and

grated spicy hard cheese, Gruyère or Parmesan

cheese for sprinkling (optional)

Salt

Pepper

1. Rub the zucchini with salt and cold water and cut into large cubes.

2. Peel the onion or shallots and garlic, chop and sauté in 3 tablespoons olive oil. Add the zucchini, season with salt and pepper.

3. Pluck the leaves from the savory and chop finely. Add the savory and sour cream to the zucchini. Steam the zucchini until firm but cooked.

4. Boil the noodles in salted water. Strain, return to the pan and mix in the remaining olive oil.

5. Arrange portions of the noodles on four plates and place the zucchini on top. Sprinkle with pumpkin-seed oil and grated cheese as desired.

Potato Noodles with Warm Cabbage Salad

Ingredients for 4 servings

2 lb mealy potatoes

11 oz coarse flour

3 eggs

1 pinch of grated nutmeg

Clarified butter for baking

1 pinch of dried wormwood

2 oz bacon

1 onion

1/2 white cabbage, finely cut

1 teaspoon caraway

About 1/2 cup vinegar (depending on the acidity)

Salt

Pepper

1. Boil the potatoes, peel them and put them through the potato masher. Mix with the flour, eggs, nutmeg, salt and pepper into a dough.

2. Form thumb-thick rolls with the dough. Cut off pieces about 3/4 inch long and fry in hot clarified butter until golden. Sprinkle dried wormwood on the noodles.

3. While the potatoes are cooking, prepare the cabbage salad: dice the bacon, peel the onion and chop. Roast the bacon and onion in 1 tablespoon clarified butter.

4. Put the cabbage into a large pan. Add the roasted bacon, onions and caraway. Bring 2 cups water with the vinegar to a boil and pour over the cabbage. Cover and allow to stand for 1/4 hour, possibly over hot water to keep it warm.

Jerusalem Artichoke Pizza

Ingredients for 6 servings

14 oz Jerusalem artichokes

1 generous cup fresh cream

1 to 2 teaspoons chopped rosemary needles

30 small olives

1 to 2 tablespoons olive oil

Salt

Pepper

For the brioche dough:

9 oz finely ground flour

3 eggs

4 oz butter

2 tablespoons milk

1 oz sugar

1/5 oz yeast

1/5 oz salt

1. Beat the ingredients for the brioche dough with a wooden spoon for about ten minutes like for spaetzle dough (the dough should be very elastic after beating). Allow the dough to stand in a cool place for about 3 hours before continuing.

2. To make the mashed Jerusalem artichokes, wash, brush and chop 7 oz artichokes. Add enough cream to cover the artichokes. Add a moderate amount of salt and pepper and boil the artichokes until they are soft.

3. Pour off part of the liquid and puree the artichokes. Put enough of the liquid back to form a creamy mass. Season with salt and pepper.

4. Cut the remaining artichokes into very thin slices. Preheat the oven to 390 °F.

5. Form the brioche dough into a large circle. Spread with pureed artichoke and slices of artichoke overlapping like a fan. Sprinkle with rosemary, scatter the olives on top and sprinkle with olive oil. Bake in the oven for 15 minutes.

K. and R. Obauer

The pizza is even tastier if thinly sliced porcini mushrooms or truffles are spread on it and porcini or truffle oil is sprinkled over it.

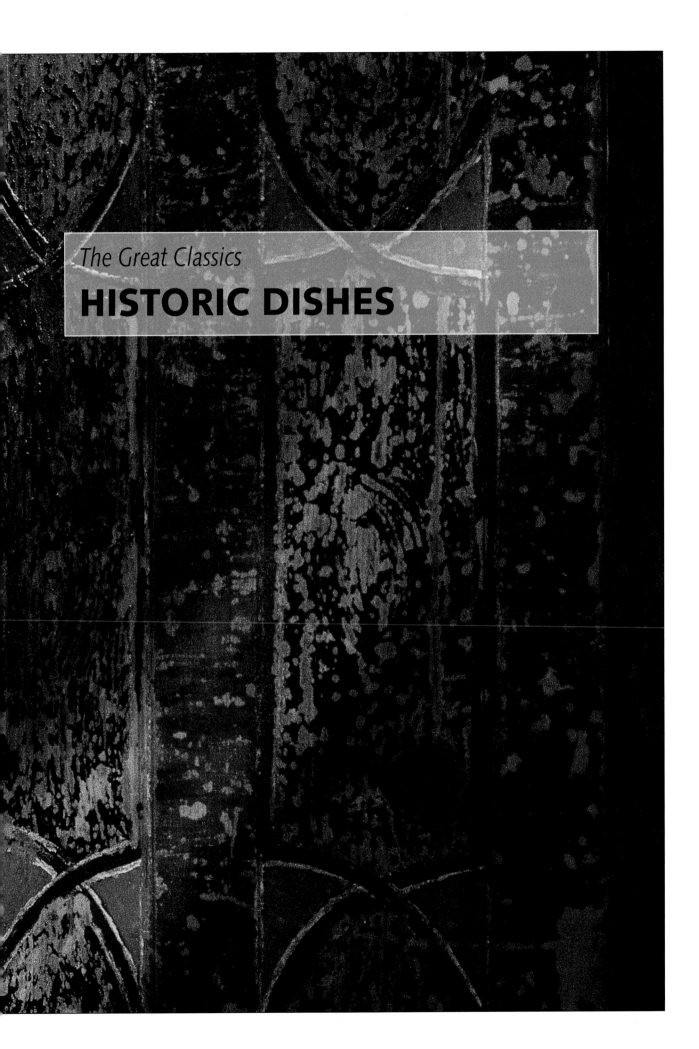

The Great Classics
HISTORIC DISHES

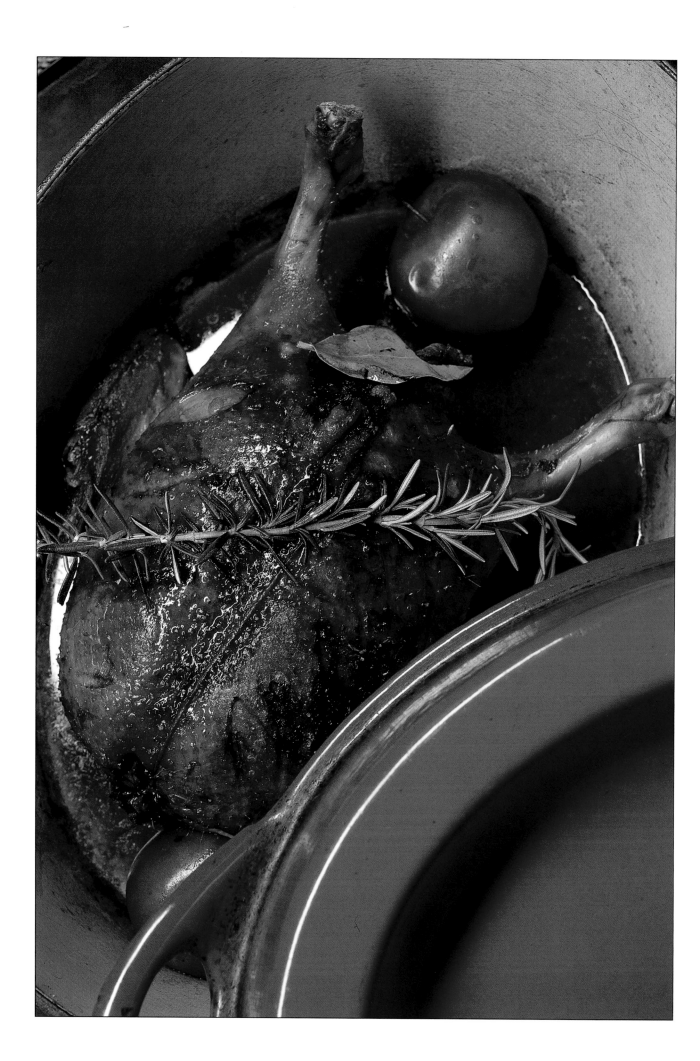

Stuffed Duck with Apple

Ingredients for 8 servings

2 ducks of about 4 1/2 lb each

A little melted butter

1 pinch of caraway

1 teaspoon dried marjoram

A little mugwort (optional)

Honey · Flour

6 tablespoons balsamic vinegar

1 generous cup red wine

A teaspoon chopped ginger and/or lemon

grass (optional)

Butter to thicken the sauce

Salt · Pepper

For the stuffing:

4 stale rolls

1 pinch of nutmeg

1 teaspoon dried marjoram

1 clove of garlic

A few dried porcini mushrooms (optional)

3/4 cup milk

1/2 onion

The duck livers

2 oz any type of mushrooms

3 1/2 oz butter

2 eggs

Salt · pepper

For the saffron or lime apples:

4 sour, firm apples

4 tablespoons sugar

2 tablespoons butter

A little saffron or lime zest

Apple juice

For the spiced honey:

2 tablespoons honey

1/2 teaspoon caraway

1/2 teaspoon ginger (chopped finely)

1 small clove of garlic

Juice and zest of 1 orange and 1 lemon

(zest very finely cut)

1/2 teaspoon black pepper · 10 rosemary needles

1. For the stuffing dice the rolls, mix with salt, pepper, nutmeg, marjoram and crushed garlic. If desired, also add 1 teaspoon ground porcini mushrooms. Pour warm milk over the mixture.

2. Peel the onion and chop with the duck livers, clean the mushrooms and cut into thin slices. Sauté the onion, livers and mushrooms in 2 to 3 tablespoons butter and mix into the bread.

3. Beat the remaining butter with the eggs and a little salt. Mix with the bread mixture. Press the mixture together and let stand.

4. Bone the ducks. Cut the skin along the back and cut or scrape the meat from both sides to the breast bone. (Remove the skin carefully along the breast bone – it should not be cut.) Cut the thigh bones out of the hip joints, remove the thigh bones; the drumstick bones remain in the meat.

5. Sew the ducks together at the front and along the back with kitchen thread. Stuff, and sew up the open ends. Brush the ducks with butter, season with salt, pepper, caraway, marjoram and possibly mugwort. Preheat the oven to 390 °F.

6. Lay the ducks in a casserole with the breast side upwards. Chop the bones and add to the ducks with a little water and roast the ducks in the preheated oven. After 1/4 hour, reduce the heat to 370 °F and roast the ducks for another 2 1/4 hours. Baste continually.

7. Mix the ingredients for the spiced honey and bring to a boil. Brush the ducks with this about 10 minutes before they finish cooking.

8. Remove the ducks from the casserole and keep warm for up to 1/2 hour; the stuffing can be cut better after standing.

9. Scoop the fat from the gravy. Sprinkle the bones and gravy with a little flour, balsamic vinegar, red wine, possibly a little chopped ginger and/or the lemon grass. Boil the gravy to reduce it to half the quantity. Strain and whisk in enough butter to make a creamy sauce. Season with salt and pepper.

10. Cut the unpeeled apples into segments, remove the core. Caramelize the sugar in butter. Toss the apple segments in the sugar and add a little saffron or grated lime zest and a dash of good apple juice. Toss again.

11. Remove the kitchen thread from the ducks. Cut the ducks into slices and serve with sauce and apples.

K. and R. Obauer

As an alternative filling, the duck can also be stuffed with pieces of bacon, halved porcini, pieces of Jerusalem artichoke, grated orange zest, pine nuts and a little cinnamon.

Soaked Rump Roast with Braised Lettuce Salad

Ingredients for 6 servings

1 rump roast, about 3 1/2 lb,
matured for at least one week

1 lb soup bones

2 onions

2 carrots

1/4 celeriac

1 bay leaf

5 peppercorns

5 coriander seeds

1 bouillon cube

1 leek

A few lovage leaves

1 pinch of ground cumin

Salt

Pepper

For the salad:

3 firm heads of lettuce (iceberg or cos lettuce)

1 generous cup fresh cream

2 mealy potatoes

1 pinch of grated nutmeg

1 clove of garlic

Salt

Pepper

1. Allow the bones to stand for 1/2 hour in cold water. Bring to a boil and pour off the water.

2. Halve the onions, peel the carrots and celeriac. Bring the bones to a boil with the onions, carrots and celeriac in a good 2 quarts of cold water. Wash the rump roast in cold water, add and bring to a boil. Scoop off froth and residue forming.

3. Add the bay leaf, peppercorns, coriander seeds and bouillon cube and allow the rump roast to simmer on a low heat for 2 1/2 to 3 hours. The rump roast has to be tender so that when pressed by the finger it leaves an impression.

4. 1/2 hour before the meat is done, bind the leek and a few lovage leaves together and put into the soup. (If the leek is not bound or is kept in too long, the soup becomes cloudy.)

5. Lift the roast out of the soup, lay in ice-cold salted water and allow to stand for at least 1/4 hour (the meat cuts better after standing).

6. In the meantime, prepare the salad: Cut the lettuce into broad strips. Heat the cream, grate a small mealy potato and add, season with salt and pepper. Season with grated nutmeg and a touch of garlic. Lay the lettuce into this, cover and bring the cream to a boil.

7. Cut the roast into slices and heat it in the soup. Serve with side dishes, season with salt, pepper and sprinkle with a little cumin.

Beef Goulash with Bread Dumplings

Ingredients for 8 servings

5 1/4 lb shin of beef	For the dumplings:
1 3/4 lb onions	1 lb diced white rolls
4 tablespoons pork drippings	1 onion
1 tablespoon sugar	1 tablespoon butter
4 tablespoons vinegar	1 pinch grated nutmeg
10 tablespoons paprika powder (mild)	1/2 to 1 tablespoon chopped parsley
1 bouillon cube	A little chopped chervil (optional)
2 bay leaves	1 tablespoon flour
3 tablespoons dried marjoram	2 eggs
1 pinch of thyme	3/4 cup milk
1/2 tablespoon ground caraway	Salt
5 cloves of garlic	Pepper
A little cornstarch (optional)	
8 tablespoons sour cream · Salt	

1. Cut the meat into cubes, peel the onions and slice thinly. Fry the onions in the drippings with sugar until golden. Pour in vinegar and add 1 1/2 quarts of water. Whisk the paprika powder in well.

2. Put the meat in, season with salt, add the bouillon cube, bay leaves, marjoram, thyme, caraway and the peeled and crushed garlic. Cover and allow to simmer on a low heat for 1 3/4 hours.

3. If the juice seems too thin, thicken it with a little cornstarch dissolved in water.

4. For the bread dumplings: Peel the onion, chop and sauté in butter. Put the diced rolls into a dish, season with salt, pepper, nutmeg, parsley and, if desired, chervil. Mix with the flour, the sautéed onion, the eggs and the warm milk. Press the mixture together and allow to stand for about 20 minutes.

5. With damp hands, form dumplings, lay these in hot salted water or hot soup, cover and allow to steep for about 10 minutes.

6. Serve the goulash with the dumplings. Put one spoonful of sour cream on each portion.

K. and R. Obauer

The right pot for making goulash is a heavy braising pot. It conducts the heat slowly and evenly. By the way, goulash tastes even better when it has been warmed up once, so ideally prepare it the day before. Polenta can also be served instead of dumplings (see photo).

Calf's Head with Sweet-and-Sour Sauce

Ingredients for 6 to 8 servings

1 small calf's head, halved by the butcher

1 carrot

1/2 celeriac

2 onions

5 peppercorns

2 pimentos

1 clove

1 bay leaf

3 shallots

3 tablespoons freshly chopped herbs

(e.g. lovage, parsley, chervil, sorrel)

1 tablespoon capers

1 tablespoon hot mustard

3 egg whites

2 eggs, a little flour and breadcrumbs for coating

1 tablespoon butter

2 tablespoons oil

Salt · Pepper

For the sauce:

2 tablespoons chopped arugola or parsley

6 tablespoons olive oil or pumpkin-seed oil

3 tablespoons balsamic vinegar

Juice of 1 lemon

2 tablespoons soy sauce

1 pinch of sugar

Salt

Pepper

1. Stand the calf's head in cold water for one day.

2. Peel the carrot, celeriac and onions. Put the calf's head into a large pot with the vegetables, salt, peppercorns, pimentos, clove and bay leaf, fill with water until the calf's head is covered and simmer for 2 to 3 hours. The calf's head is ready when the meat in the cheek can be pushed out easily. Allow to cool, remove the meat from the bones.

3. Preheat the oven to 340 °F. Peel and chop the shallots. Mix the light meat with the shallots, herbs, capers, mustard, salt and pepper well, beat the egg whites with a fork and mix in. Put into a terrine mold and cook standing in water in the preheated oven for 1/2 hour. Allow to cool and remove from the mold.

4. Cut the calf's head into slices and coat each slice with breadcrumbs one side like a schnitzel. To do this, beat the egg. Dust the slices of meat with flour, dip in the beaten egg and press into the breadcrumbs. Heat the butter and oil in a pan. Fry the calf's head on the coated side in a covered pan or the oven for about 5 minutes.

5. For the sauce: Wash the arugola or parsley and chop. Mix with the remaining ingredients.

6. Serve the calf's head with the sauce and new potatoes or wild garlic and potato salad.

Creamed Veal with Asparagus, Cress and New Potatoes

Ingredients for 4 servings

2 lb veal hocks

Crushed white pepper

1 pinch of grated nutmeg

1 to 2 tablespoons peanut oil

4 shallots

1 generous cup white wine

1 pinch saffron or 1/2 teaspoon ground turmeric

(optional)

1 bay leaf

20 small, new potatoes, about 11 oz

1 teaspoon caraway

8 stalks of asparagus, about 12 oz

1 generous cup fresh cream

Butter for thickening the sauce

A little watercress to garnish

Salt

Pepper

1. Dice the meat, season with salt, crushed pepper and nutmeg. Sprinkle with oil.

2. Peel the shallots and chop coarsely. Put the meat and the shallots into a braising pot and sauté. Add the wine and 1 generous cup of water. Add the nutmeg, saffron or turmeric and the bay leaf. Cover the meat and braise for 1 1/2 hours until the meat is almost tender.

3. Steam the potatoes over water containing caraway and peel.

4. Peel the asparagus and cut off the woody ends. Cut the asparagus into lengths of about 2 inches and put in with the meat about 10 minutes before it is done. Pour in the cream.

5. Lift the meat and asparagus out of the pot. Strain the juice. Whisk in enough butter to make a creamy sauce. Season the sauce with salt and pepper.

6. Put the potatoes, asparagus and veal hock into a dish, pour over the sauce and serve sprinkled with cress.

Wiener Schnitzel with Parsley Potatoes and Salad

Ingredients for 4 servings

4 veal schnitzel from the back

(just over 1/3 inch thick and weighing 5 1/2 oz)

Flour

2 eggs

White breadcrumbs

2 to 3 tablespoons vegetable oil

1 tablespoon pork drippings

Salt

Pepper

For the parsley potatoes:

11 oz oval, firm potatoes

1 tablespoon butter

1 to 2 tablespoons chopped parsley

Salt

For the salad:

Lettuce

4 tablespoons cider vinegar

4 tablespoons white wine

1 tablespoon soy sauce

1 dash of Worcester sauce

1/2 tablespoon sugar

4 tablespoons sunflower or olive oil

1 to 2 tablespoons freshly chopped herbs

(e.g. lemon balm, basil, chervil, arugola, parsley)

A little coarsely grated Parmesan cheese

(optional)

Salt

1. Steam and peel the potatoes.

2. Gently pound the schnitzel, season with salt and pepper. Toss in flour, dip in beaten eggs and then into white breadcrumbs. Press the breadcrumbs on gently and shake off loose ones.

3. Fry the schnitzel in a generous amount of vegetable oil with drippings until golden. Important: the fat has to be hot enough to bubble and spit gently when a Schnitzel is put in. Fat that is too hot prevents the coating from rising.

4. As soon as the schnitzel has browned underneath, turn over and finish frying (altogether about 7 minutes). Remove the schnitzel from the fat and allow to drain on paper towel.

5. Pour the fat from frying the schnitzel out of the pan, except for a small quantity, add the butter and heat. Brown the potatoes in this. Add the parsley, toss the potatoes and season with salt.

6. For the salad: Prepare a marinade with the vinegar, white wine, soy sauce, Worcester sauce, salt, sugar and oil.

7. Wash the lettuce and tear into small pieces. Season with salt and mix with the herbs and the marinade. If desired, sprinkle with a little Parmesan cheese.

8. Serve the schnitzel with the potatoes, salad and possibly cranberries.

K. and R. Obauer

The best meat for Wiener Schnitzel is veal from the back. Wonderful schnitzel can also be made from the fricandeau cut.

Boned Goose with Mushrooms

Ingredients for 6 to 8 servings

1 goose of about 7 1/2 to 8 lb

Butter for brushing

1 pinch of caraway

1 to 2 teaspoons dried marjoram

1 to 2 tablespoons liquid honey

1/2 to 1 tablespoon flour

5 tablespoons balsamic vinegar

1 generous cup red wine

Salt

Pepper

For the filling:

4 stale rolls

1 pinch of grated nutmeg

1 teaspoon dried marjoram

A little dried mugwort (optional)

1 clove of garlic

A small quantity of dried porcini (optional)

3/4 cup milk

1/2 onion

The goose liver

2 oz mushrooms or porcini

3 1/2 oz butter

2 eggs

Salt

Pepper

1. For the filling: Dice the rolls and season with salt, pepper, nutmeg, marjoram, mugwort if desired, and the crushed clove of garlic. Possibly also stir in 1 teaspoon of porcini "powder", i.e. dried and ground porcini. Cover with the warm milk and mix.

2. Chop the onion and liver from the goose, cut a few mushrooms of any sort into fine slices. Sauté the onion, liver and mushrooms in a little butter and mix this into the diced bread.

3. Beat the remaining butter (room temperature) with the eggs and a little salt and mix into the bread. Press the mixture together and let stand.

4. Bone the goose. Cut the skin along the back and finely cut or scrape the meat to the breast bone on both sides. (Remove the skin carefully along the breast bone, preferably with the fingers – it should not be cut.) Cut the thigh bones out of the hip joints, remove the thigh bones; the drumstick bones remain in the meat.

5. Preheat the oven to 430 °F. Sew the goose together at the front and along the back with kitchen thread. Stuff, and sew up the open end. Brush the goose with butter, season with salt, pepper, caraway and dried marjoram.

6. Chop the bones, the best way is to use kitchen scissors. Put them into a casserole, lay the goose with the breast upwards on them, add a little water and roast in the oven for 1/4 hour. Reduce the heat to 370 °F and allow to roast for another 3 hours. Baste continually. Brush with honey about 10 minutes before it is done.

7. Remove the goose from the casserole and keep warm. Ideally, the goose should be finished 1/2 to 1 hour before serving and be able to stand at a temperature of about 140 °F, e.g. in the warm oven, switched off with the door slightly open.

8. Scoop the fat from the gravy. Sprinkle the bones and gravy with a little flour, balsamic vinegar, red wine. Boil the gravy to reduce it by half. Strain. Season with salt and pepper.

9. Remove the kitchen thread from the goose. Cut the goose into slices and serve with the sauce.

K. and R. Obauer

This is the best way to roast a goose without stuffing to make it crispy: Put the goose into a little water and roast for approx. 1/2 hour at 450 °F. Reduce the heat to 340 °F and roast for another 2 to 3 hours. Wrap the goose in cloth or aluminum foil and leave to stand in the oven (switched off) for 1 to 2 hours. Divide the goose into breast and legs and heat these pieces again at 450 °F for about 1/4 hour.

Onion Roast

Ingredients for 4 servings

4 onions

A little flour

Vegetable oil for frying

4 slices of roast beef with fat, just over 1/2 inch

thick and matured for at least 2 weeks

A little mustard

1 tablespoon pork drippings

1 dash of beef soup or red wine

1 dash of balsamic vinegar (optional)

1 to 2 tablespoons cold butter

Salt · Pepper

1. Peel the onions, cut into slices as thick as the back of the knife blade, season with salt and toss in flour. Fry in hot vegetable oil until golden. Remove the onions from the pan and allow to drain on paper towel. Careful: the onions continue browning once they are out of the pan, so take them out in time!

2. Gently flatten the meat, score the fat. Season the meat with salt and pepper. Spread mustard on one side and dip this side in flour.

3. Heat the drippings and an equal amount of oil in a pan. Briefly fry the meat with the flour side down, turn, cover, fry for about 7 minutes.

4. Lift the meat out of the pan and keep warm. Dust the juice with flour, pour in a dash of soup or red wine and whisk in the cold butter. Strain the juice, season with salt, pepper and, if liked, a dash of balsamic vinegar.

5. Serve the roast with onions and sauce. Fried potatoes go well with this.

Pork Rice

Ingredients for 4 servings

1 1/2 lb pork, from leg fillet or spare rib

2 onions

3 tablespoons pork drippings

3 cups beef stock

1 bay leaf

3 tablespoons paprika powder (mild)

3 cloves of garlic

1 pinch of cayenne pepper

1 pinch of ground caraway

1 1/2 cups of long-grained rice

A piece of ham rind and a piece of Parmesan

cheese rind (optional)

2 red bell peppers

2 pickles

2 chili peppers (optional)

2 oz grated Parmesan cheese

1 tablespoon freshly chopped herbs (e.g.

chervil, wild garlic, chives, marjoram, 1 sage leaf)

Salt

Pepper

1. Cut the meat into very thin slices. Peel and chop the onions.

2. Fry the onions and meat in the pork drippings and pour on the soup. Add the bay leaf, paprika powder, peeled and crushed garlic, cayenne pepper, caraway and rice. If desired, add the ham and Parmesan rind. Allow to simmer for 1/2 hour on very low heat.

3. Wash and halve the bell peppers, remove the seeds and ribs and dice. Chop the peppers, the pickles and the chili peppers, if desired. Shortly before the rice is ready, mix in the diced red bell peppers, pickles and chili peppers.

4. Remove the ham and Parmesan rind. Season the pork rice with salt and sprinkle with Parmesan cheese and herbs. Salad goes well with this dish.

K. and R. Obauer

The pork rice also tastes very nice if chopped capers are sprinkled over it or a little olive oil added prior to serving.

Stuffed Peppers

Ingredients for 4 servings

8 medium-sized green peppers

3 shallots

4 tablespoons butter

1/2 cup long-grained rice

1 small onion

12 oz ground shoulder of pork or spare rib

1 generous cup sour cream

1 pinch of cayenne pepper

1 clove of garlic

1 tablespoon mustard

1/2 cup milk

1 tablespoon freshly chopped herbs

(e.g. sorrel or parsley)

30 cocktail tomatoes or 6 beef tomatoes

1 bunch of basil

1 sprig of mint

1 tablespoon tomato paste

Salt · Pepper

1. Cut off the peppers' caps, remove the seeds and ribs.

2. Peel the shallots and chop. Sauté in 2 table-spoons of butter, add the long-grained rice and steam until transparent. Add not quite a cup of water, season with salt and steam the rice.

3. Peel the onion, chop into small pieces and sauté in 1 tablespoon of butter.

4. Mix the meat with 2 tablespoons of sour cream, the rice, onion, salt, pepper, cayenne pepper, the crushed garlic clove, mustard, a little milk and the herbs into a soft mass. Fill the peppers with the mass. Preheat the oven to 370 °F.

5. Remove the core from the tomatoes. Put into a sufficiently high pot (the lid has to fit after the peppers are put in) with the basil, mint, remaining butter, tomato paste and the rest of the sour cream. Season with salt and put the peppers into the pot but not too close together. Put into the oven, cover and steam for 1 1/2 hours.

6. Remove the peppers from the pot. Briefly puree the mixture with a hand blender, if desired, press through a sieve. Season with salt and pepper to taste and serve the peppers with the sauce.

Szeged Goulash

Ingredients for 8 servings

2 1/2 lb breast of pork, spare rib or shoulder

3 onions

3 tablespoons pork drippings

1/2 tablespoon sugar

5 cloves of garlic

3 tablespoons vinegar

7 tablespoons paprika powder (mild)

1 chili pepper · 1 bay leaf

3 juniper berries · 1 teaspoon caraway

5 peppercorns

A few sprigs of savory (optional)

1 1/2 lb firm potatoes

12 oz sauerkraut

8 tablespoons sour cream

A little freshly chopped marjoram or wild garlic

(optional)

Salt

1. Cut the meat into cubes of almost 1 inch. Peel the onions and cut into fine slices, sauté in drippings and sugar.

2. Peel and crush the garlic cloves and stir into the onions, pour in the vinegar and add 1 1/2 quarts water or soup. Season with salt, paprika powder, chopped chili pepper, bay leaf, juniper berries, caraway, peppercorns, if desired, the savory, and add the meat. Cover and allow to simmer for about 1/2 hour.

3. Peel the potatoes and cut into walnut-sized pieces. Mix the potatoes and sauerkraut with the meat, cover and cook for about another 45 minutes.

4. Ladle the goulash onto plates and top each portion with a good spoonful of sour cream. Possibly sprinkle with marjoram or wild garlic.

Venison Ragout

Ingredients for 8 servings

5 1/2 lb leg of venison

4 tablespoons pork drippings

2 carrots

3 onions

1/4 celeriac

1 oz ginger

1 cup cranberries

1 cup blueberries

1 cup red wine marc

5 tablespoons sugar

5 1/2 oz smoked bacon

A good 2 quarts strong red wine

2 teaspoons dark chocolate

3 juniper berries

10 coriander seeds

1/2 tablespoon caraway

4 cloves of garlic

1 shot of herb liqueur (Bénédictine or Chartreuse)

1 pinch of dried wormwood

Butter to thicken the sauce

A little cornstarch (optional)

Salt

Pepper

1. Cut the meat into 1 1/2 inches cubes. Melt the drippings in a large braising pan, sauté the meat, season with salt and pepper, cover and braise until the juice from the meat has evaporated.

2. Peel and dice the carrots, peel the onions and cut into segments. Peel the celeriac and dice, slice the ginger finely (the peel can remain on).

3. Add the vegetables, cranberries, blueberries, optional red wine marc, sugar and the piece of bacon to the meat. Add the wine. Stir in a piece of dark chocolate, the juniper berries, coriander seeds, caraway or cumin, the peeled and crushed cloves of garlic, herb liqueur and, if desired the wormwood. Cover the ragout and allow to simmer for about 2 hours.

4. Lift the meat out of the ragout. Pour the sauce through a sieve, reheat and whisk in a few tablespoons of butter to thicken, if necessary stir in a little cornstarch dissolved in wine. Season the sauce with salt and pepper, put the meat into the sauce.

5. Serve the venison ragout preferably with celeriac puree (see page 112–113) or with cream polenta (make the polenta from equal quantities of milk and cream).

Soaked Shin with Pumpkin and Turmeric

Ingredients for 6 servings

4 lb well-matured shin of beef

4 onions

2 carrots

1/4 celeriac

1 parsnip

A little savory

4 cloves of garlic

1 bay leaf

5 peppercorns

5 coriander seeds

1 bouillon cube

1 leek

A few lovage leaves

6 mealy potatoes

1 tablespoon butter

1 3/4 lb pumpkin (preferably Hokkaido)

1 pinch ground turmeric

A little cornstarch

2 to 3 tablespoons freshly chopped seasonal

herbs (e.g. parsley, dill, chervil, chives)

1 dash of vinegar

Salt

Pepper

1. Put the meat into about 2 quarts of simmering water. Bring the water to a boil, remove froth and residue.

2. Add 2 halved onions, peeled carrots, peeled celeriac, parsnip, a little savory, 2 unpeeled cloves of garlic, bay leaf, peppercorns, coriander seeds and bouillon cube and simmer for 2 1/2 to 3 hours on a low heat. The shin has to be tender enough for the bone to separate easily from the meat.

3. 1/2 hour before the meat is done, tie the leek and a few leaves of lovage together and add to the soup (if the leek is not tied or remains in the soup for too long the soup will become cloudy).

4. Peel the potatoes and cut into thick slices. Chop the remaining onions and sauté in butter. Add 2 crushed cloves of garlic and pour in 2 cups soup. Add the slices of potato and boil in the soup until almost tender.

5. Peel the pumpkin and cut into large cubes. Cut the vegetables boiled in the soup (not the leek) into small pieces and put into the potato slices with the pumpkin and a little turmeric.

6. Bring everything to a boil and thicken the liquid with a little cornstarch. Stir in lots of seasonal herbs, season with salt and pepper and a little vinegar. Serve the vegetables with the shin.

Leg of Lamb with Beans

Ingredients for 6 servings

5 1/2 oz scarlet runner beans

1 piece of ham rind (optional)

1 well-matured leg of lamb weighing

4 to 4 1/2 lb (without the shank)

7 tablespoons olive oil

5 tablespoons chopped olives

1 tablespoon chopped rosemary

A few chopped sage leaves

12 cloves of garlic

A little hyssop

1 generous cup dry white wine

6 beef tomatoes or 9 oz cocktail tomatoes

Salt · Pepper

1. Soak the beans in water for 24 hours.

2. If available, add a piece of ham rind to the beans and bring to a boil in the water used for soaking. Boil the beans for about 1 hour until they are almost tender. Strain the beans.

3. Take the large bone out of the leg of lamb. Grind a paste from 5 tablespoons olive oil, the chopped olives, chopped rosemary, chopped sage leaves, three peeled and crushed garlic cloves and a little hyssop using the pestle and mortar. Brush the inside of the leg with this paste.

4. Preheat the oven to 430 °F. Tie the leg up with kitchen thread, rub outside with salt, pepper, three peeled and crushed garlic cloves and olive oil.

5. Lay the leg of lamb in a braising pot with 6 unpeeled garlic cloves and roast in the oven. Reduce the heat to 370 °F after 1/2 hour and add the wine. Baste the leg continually with the juice.

6. Wash the tomatoes, core and cut into quarters. After 45 minutes, add the beans and tomatoes to the meat. Braise everything for another 1/4 hour. Switch the oven off and allow the leg of lamb to stand for another 1/2 hour.

7. Lift the meat out of the pot and cut into thin slices. Arrange on plates, sprinkle with olive oil, perhaps also with a herb mixture (see page 21). Serve with the tomato and bean ragout.

Roasted Goat Kid

Ingredients for 4 servings

1 1/2 lb filleted, well-matured kid meat

3 deep dishes, 1 with milk, 1 with flour and

1 with white breadcrumbs

2 eggs

Clarified butter for frying

5 tablespoons sour cream

1 tablespoon mustard

1 untreated lime

5 tablespoons cress

1 bunch of parsley or dandelion

Salt · Pepper

1. Cut the meat into small cutlets, gently pound, season with salt and pepper. Dip in the milk, then the flour, in beaten eggs and then in breadcrumbs to coat.

2. Fry the cutlets floating in clarified butter until golden.

3. Mix a sauce from the sour cream, mustard, grated lime zest and cress.

4. Serve the kid with the sauce and parsley or dandelion fried in clarified butter. Sprinkle with lemon or lime juice.

Rack of Venison with Celeriac Puree and Wormwood Sauce

Ingredients for 4 servings

1 rack of venison, about 4 1/2 lb

1/4 celeriac

1 carrot

2 lb venison bones, chopped by the butcher

into small pieces

2 tablespoons butter

2 oz bacon

A piece of ham rind (optional)

2 tablespoons sugar

1/2 bulb of garlic

Generous 4 cups red burgundy

2 oz blueberries

2 oz cranberries

2 oz marc (optional)

1 pinch of wormwood

1 good shot of herb liqueur (e.g. Chartreuse or

Bénédictine)

2 teaspoons dark chocolate

1 tablespoon finely chopped ginger

3 juniper berries

1/2 teaspoon caraway

Oil for frying

A little cornstarch (optional)

Salt · Pepper

For the celeriac puree:

1 celeriac

1 mealy potato

1/2 cup milk

1/2 cup fresh cream

Salt

Pepper

1. Cut the fillets out of the rack of venison. Peel the celeriac and carrot and cut into pieces. Sauté the vegetables and the bones in butter, add and also sauté the bacon, if desired a piece of ham rind, sugar and the unpeeled bulb of garlic.

2. Add the wine, blueberries, cranberries, marc, wormwood, herb liqueur, a piece of dark chocolate, ginger, juniper berries and caraway. Allow to simmer for about 3 hours without a lid. Add water to replace what has evaporated.

3. Pour the stock through a sieve and boil until the liquid is reduced to about a generous cup. Whisk in a little butter and possibly thicken the sauce with cornstarch.

4. Cut each venison fillet into four pieces, season with salt and pepper. Fry for a total of 8 minutes on both sides in a mixture of oil and butter.

5. Lift the meat out of the pan, pour away the fat. Put the sauce back into the pan and allow the meat to steep in the sauce for a few minutes.

6. For the celeriac puree: Peel and chop the celeriac and potato. Add equal amounts of milk and cream to just cover the vegetables, season moderately with salt and pepper and boil until the celeriac is very soft.

7. Pour away part of the liquid and puree the vegetables with a hand blender. Add enough of the boiled liquid to provide a creamy puree. Season with salt and pepper.

8. Serve the venison on the celeriac puree.

K. and R. Obauer

A sauce to go well with game dishes can be made with few ingredients: Boil 2 cups of good red wine with a few crushed peppercorns, 2 tablespoons of sugar and approx. 10 finely chopped shallots to concentrate the liquid (it takes approx. 1/2 hour). Thicken with very little potato starch or cornstarch, if desired.

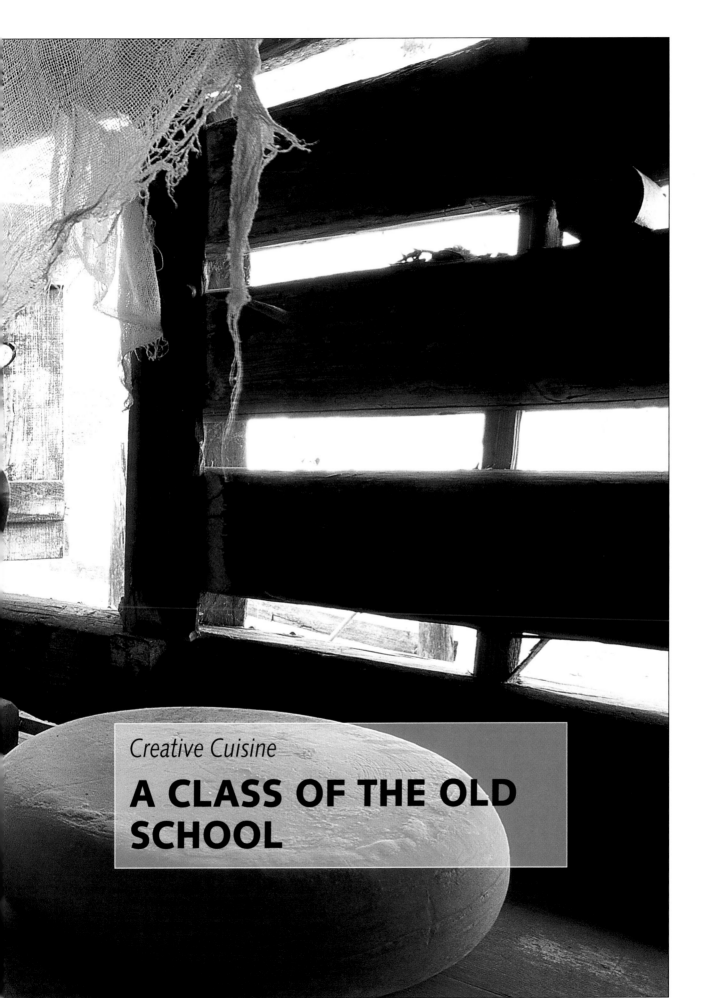

Creative Cuisine

A CLASS OF THE OLD SCHOOL

Chicken with Ginger and Soy Sauce in Rice Pastry

Ingredients for 4 servings

4 chicken breast fillets (breasts from

2 chickens, skinned)

1 clove of garlic

5 coriander seeds

1 untreated lemon

2 tablespoons freshly cut lovage, chervil and

mint, possibly also wild garlic

1 teaspoon brown sugar

1 teaspoon ginger

1 tablespoon peanut oil

1 tablespoon soy sauce

8 leaves of rice pastry (diameter 10 inches,

from shops with Asian foods)

1 tablespoon rice flour

A good quantity of vegetable oil for frying

4 spring onions

1 carrot

3 1/2 oz green beans

2 oz bean sprouts

2 tablespoons peanut oil

Salt · Pepper

For the sauce:

2 carrots

2 cloves of garlic

4 shallots

2 oz ginger

3 tablespoons brown sugar

2 cups chicken stock

1 sprig of rosemary

5 coriander seeds

A little lovage

4 tablespoons soy sauce

A little rice flour for thickening

1. First prepare the sauce: Peel the carrots, garlic and shallots and cut into fine slices. Cut the ginger into fine slices. Boil with the sugar, chicken stock, rosemary, coriander seeds, lovage and soy sauce until reduced to half the quantity. Strain the stock and thicken with a little rice flour dissolved in water.

2. Cut the chicken breasts in two lengthways and mix with the crushed garlic and coriander seeds, the grated lemon zest, lovage, chervil, mint, if desired, chopped wild garlic, the brown sugar, chopped ginger, peanut oil and soy sauce.

3. Soak the rice pastry in cold water, remove from the water and spread the sheets out on a dish towel. Lay the chicken on the pastry lengthways. Mix the rice flour with a little water, brush on the empty side of the pastry. Roll the pastry up from the unbrushed side and press the ends together.

4. Fry the rice roll floating in vegetable oil for about 8 minutes while continually basting it with the oil. Remove from the fat and dab dry.

5. Clean the spring onions and cut into lengths just over 1 inch. Peel the carrot and cut into julienne strips. Prepare the beans, blanche them and cut into lengths just over 1 inch long. Wash the bean sprouts.

6. Heat the peanut oil in a pan. First briefly fry the carrot and spring onions, then toss the green beans and the bean sprouts in the oil. Add 3 tablespoons sauce and season with salt and pepper.

7. Arrange the vegetables on a plate, lay the chicken in rice pastry on top and add the sauce.

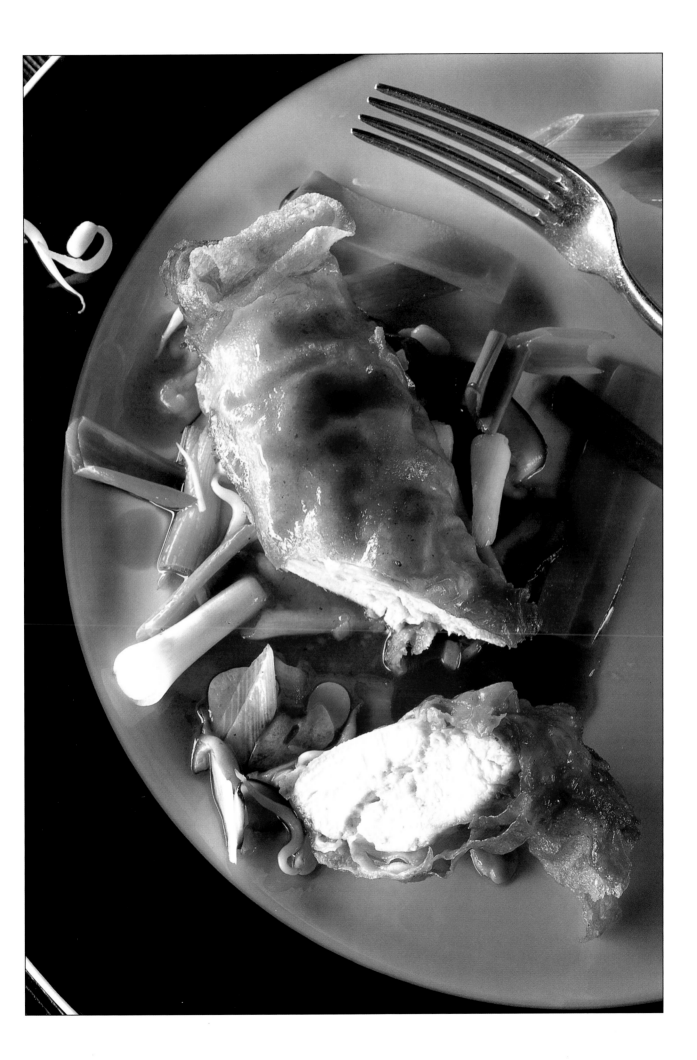

Chicken with Red Peppers

Ingredients for 4 servings

4 chicken legs

8 red bell peppers

2 cups olive oil

5 cloves of garlic

1 sprig of rosemary

1 teaspoon chopped rosemary needles

A little balsamic vinegar

A little fennel green (optional)

1 pinch of cumin (optional)

Salt

Crushed black pepper

1. Halve the peppers, remove the seeds and halve again. Heat a generous amount of olive oil. Simmer the peppers and the unpeeled garlic cloves for about 1/2 hour. Remove the peppers from the fat and pull off the skin.

2. Bone the chicken legs, cut each into three pieces (the skin is not removed). Preheat the oven to 390 °F.

3. Heat a little olive oil in an ovenproof dish. Lay the meat inside skin down and fry quickly. Add the sprig of rosemary, put the dish in the oven and roast the meat for about 8 minutes.

4. Arrange the peppers on 4 plates, lay the chicken on top and pour the fat from the pan over them, sprinkle with rosemary and crushed black pepper, season with salt and sprinkle with balsamic vinegar. If available, sprinkle fennel green and ground cumin as desired.

K. and R. Obauer

Breast of chicken (without skin) can be used instead of legs. Take the breast fillets out a little earlier.

Chicken Breast with Mashed Potatoes

Ingredients for 4 servings

4 chicken breasts
2 oz butter
3 olives
8 tablespoons mashed potatoes
2 oz Parmesan cheese
8 small carrots
2 oz celeriac
4 cloves of garlic
4 shallots
1 teaspoon dried marjoram
1 pinch dried wormwood
1/2 cup red wine
1/2 cup stock or brown chicken stock
Salt
Pepper

1. Skin the chicken breasts. Season with salt and pepper and quickly brown on both sides in 1 oz butter.

2. Chop the olives and mix with the mashed potatoes.

3. Use the remaining butter to grease an ovenproof casserole. Lay the chicken breasts inside, spread over mashed potatoes and sprinkle with Parmesan cheese.

4. Preheat the oven to 430 °F. Peel the carrots, celeriac, cloves of garlic and shallots. Cut the celeriac into sticks.

5. Add the vegetables with the marjoram and a little wormwood to the chicken, pour over red wine and stock. Bake in the preheated over for 12 to 14 minutes.

Veal Goulash with Curd Noodles and Deep-Fried Red Peppers

Ingredients for 4 servings

For the goulash:

2 shins of veal, a total of about 1 3/4 lb

3 onions

2 tablespoons corn oil or veal suet

1 to 2 teaspoons sugar

1 tablespoon vinegar

5 to 7 tablespoons mild paprika powder

1 pinch of cayenne pepper

1 bay leaf

1 lime

A little cornstarch (optional)

1 red bell pepper

Olive oil for frying

Salt

For the curd noodles:

9 oz noodle dough (see page 23)

5 tablespoons curds

1 egg yolk

1 lime

A few mint leaves

3 to 4 tablespoons butter

1 tablespoon freshly chopped herbs

(e.g. parsley, chervil)

Salt

Pepper

1. Peel the onions and chop finely, fry until golden brown in oil or suet. Add the sugar, pour in the vinegar and add 4 generous cups of water. Whisk in the paprika powder.

2. Cut the veal shins into large pieces and add. Season with cayenne pepper, bay leaf and salt. Cover and simmer for 1 to 1 1/4 hours.

3. Finally, add the lime zest. Thicken the goulash as desired with a little cornstarch mixed with water.

4. Wash the red pepper, halve it, remove the seeds and cut into strips or squares. Deep-fry in olive oil until soft.

5. For the curd noodles: Mix the curds well with the egg yolk, grated lime zest, chopped mint, salt and pepper. Roll out the dough until thin and cut into pieces measuring 2 x 6 inches.

6. Pipe the curd mass onto the pastry using an icing bag. Fold the pastry over lengthways and press the edges together.

7. Simmer the noodles in salted water for 3 minutes, remove and toss in butter and herbs.

8. Serve the goulash with the curd noodles and deep-fried red pepper.

Creamed Calf's Lung with Mushrooms

Ingredients for 10 servings

1 calf's lung of about 4 lb

1 calf's heart

2 bay leaves

1 tablespoon black peppercorns

1 teaspoon coriander

1 clove

1 bouillon cube

5 onions

2 tablespoons drippings

4 tablespoons oil

2 oz parsley stalks

5 pickles

4 tablespoons flour

4 tablespoons tarragon vinegar

2 cups Riesling wine

4 tablespoons pickle juice

1/2 tube anchovy paste

2 tablespoons capers

5 tablespoons tarragon mustard

3 tablespoons dried marjoram

1/2 tablespoon ground caraway

A little grated nutmeg

3 tablespoons liquid soup spice

3 1/2 oz spicy blue cheese (e.g. Gorgonzola)

3 tablespoons finely chopped herbs (lovage,

tarragon, parsley, hyssop, coriander leaves,

chives)

A generous 1 1/2 lb mushrooms

(e. g. chanterelles)

1 generous cup fresh cream

2 tablespoons butter or clarified butter

Salt · Pepper

1. Remove the tubes from the lung. Halve the heart. Soak the lung and heart in cold water for about 1/2 day and repeatedly change the water.

2. Put the lung and heart into a pot of cold water and bring to a boil. Add the bay leaf, peppercorns, coriander, clove, salt and the bouillon cube, cover and allow to simmer for 1 1/2 hours.

3. Remove the lung and heart from the stock, rinse with cold water and allow to cool. Measure 4 generous cups of stock and put aside.

4. Clean the lung, cut out large blood vessels and pipes. Cut the lung and heart into fine slices.

5. Peel and finely chop 3 onions, fry until golden brown in drippings and oil. Chop the parsley stalks, cut the pickles into fine slices and add both to the onions.

6. Stir in the flour, pour in the tarragon vinegar, Riesling, pickle juice and the lung stock. Stir in the anchovy paste, capers, tarragon mustard, marjoram, caraway, nutmeg, soup spice and the blue cheese. Bring to a boil and puree with a hand blender. Allow to boil for 10 minutes.

7. Add the lung and again bring to a boil. Stir in the finely chopped herbs, pour in the fresh cream and again bring to a boil.

8. Season with salt, pepper and possibly a dash of vinegar to create a tangy, sour flavor.

9. Serve with fried chanterelles, for example. Clean the chanterelles, peel the 2 remaining onions and chop. Fry the onions and chanterelles in a generous amount of butter (even better: clarified butter). Season with salt and pepper. Serve in deep dishes, one half lung, the other half chanterelles.

Veal with Sour Tuna Cream and Tomato Salad

Ingredients for 4 servings

4 slices veal loin (5 1/2 oz each)	20 black olives
1 tablespoon capers	Butter
A few chopped rosemary needles	Salt · Pepper
2 to 3 sage leaves, chopped	For the tomato salad:
4 tablespoons olive oil	6 beef tomatoes or 30 cherry tomatoes
1 tuna fillet of 5 1/2 oz	5 basil leaves
1 clove of garlic	5 mint leaves
1 tablespoon anchovy paste	1 lemon
4 tablespoons sour cream	5 coriander seeds
2 tablespoons crème fraîche	4 tablespoons olive oil
1/2 cup white wine	1 teaspoon sugar
1 to 2 tablespoons freshly chopped herbs	Salt · Pepper
(oregano, basil and chervil)	

1. Season the veal with salt and pepper and sprinkle with the chopped capers, rosemary, sage, 1 tablespoon of olive oil and steam over hot water for 8 to 10 minutes.

2. Cut the tuna into small pieces, sauté with the remaining capers and the crushed garlic in 3 tablespoons olive oil. Stir in the anchovy paste, sour cream, crème fraîche, white wine, a little chopped oregano and basil. Beat the mixture with a hand blender.

3. Spread the tuna cream on plates. Cut the veal into thin slices, lay on the cream and sprinkle with olives, oregano, basil and chervil.

4. For the tomato salad: Slit the tomatoes at the top and bottom, put briefly into boiling water, skin and remove the seeds. Save the juice.

5. Coarsely cut 5 basil and 5 mint leaves and squeeze the lemon.

6. Cut the tomato flesh into segments, mix with the tomato juice, crushed coriander, basil and mint, salt, pepper, olive oil, sugar and lemon juice.

K. and R. Obauer

This dish can be enjoyed hot or cold.
It resembles vitello tonnato,
but tastes even better.

Veal Hock with Fennel

Ingredients for 4 servings

1 hind veal hock of about 4 lb (matured for one week)
A little grated nutmeg
1/2 cup peanut oil
1 sprig of rosemary
A few sage leaves
1/2 cup sweet wine (e. g. white port)
1/2 cup veal stock or chicken soup
1 fennel
2 large potatoes
A few black truffles (optional)
Salt · Crushed white pepper

1. Preheat the oven to 460 °F. Rub the meat with salt, pepper and nutmeg. Put it into an ovenproof dish, pour over peanut oil, add the sprig of rosemary and the sage leaves and roast in the oven for 20 minutes.

2. Pour in the wine and veal stock or chicken soup and reduce the heat to 390 °F. Clean the fennel and halve it. Peel and halve the potatoes. After 1 hour, put the vegetables in with the hock.

3. Baste the hock repeatedly while it is roasting. If necessary, add a little water. The cooking time depends on the quality of the meat and the maturing time. It is between 2 1/2 and 3 1/2 hours.

4. Take the hock and vegetables out of the dish. Strain the gravy and season with salt and pepper. If desired, stir in chopped black truffles.

5. Remove the bone, cut into portions and serve with the vegetables and gravy.

Lamb Lung with Curry

Ingredients for 6 servings

2 lamb lungs and 2 lamb hearts, about 2 lb total

2 1/2 onions

1 carrot

1 bay leaf

2 juniper berries

1 clove

1 1/2 bulbs of garlic

5 tablespoons butter

4 tablespoons flour

1/2 cup pickle juice

4 tablespoons balsamic vinegar

1/2 cup spicy white wine (e.g. Traminer)

2 tablespoons curry

1 pinch of cayenne pepper

1/2 cup fresh cream

2 oz blue cheese (Roquefort is best)

2 tablespoons freshly chopped herbs

(e.g. celery leaves, rosemary, basil, lovage, mint,

parsley, chervil)

Salt

1. Cut the lamb hearts apart. Remove the air tubes from the lungs. Soak the lungs and hearts in cold water for one hour.

2. Put the lungs and hearts into a pot with a generous 2 quarts of fresh water. Add 1/2 peeled onion, peeled carrot, bay leaf, juniper berries, clove and half of an unpeeled garlic bulb. Moderately salt the water, bring to a boil, cover and simmer for 1 hour.

3. Remove the meat from the stock and place it in cold water. As soon as it is cold, take it out and cut out the large blood veins with a sharp knife. Cut the trimmed meat into fine strips.

4. Peel the two onions, chop finely and fry until golden in butter. Mix in 3 peeled and crushed garlic cloves, dust with flour and pour in the pickle juice and the balsamic vinegar.

5. Pour in 2 cups stock and wine. Stir in curry, a little cayenne pepper and the fresh cream. Simmer the sauce for 10 minutes. Add the blue cheese and beat the sauce with a hand blender.

6. Cut the carrot from the stock into small pieces. Stir the carrot, meat and herbs into the sauce.

K. and R. Obauer

*Serve the lamb lungs with white bread
or polenta.*

Oxtail in Mashed Potato

Ingredients for 6 servings

1 oxtail (have it cut into slices by the butcher)

1 slice of bacon

4 tablespoons olive oil

2 carrots

1 head of celery

2 onions

A generous 2 quarts of red wine

1 teaspoon tomato paste

1 sprig of thyme

1 sprig of rosemary

2 cloves

8 peppercorns

2 cloves of garlic

14 oz mealy potatoes

1/2 teaspoon caraway

4 tablespoons milk · 3 1/2 oz butter

3 1/2 oz mushrooms (best: porcini)

6 shallots

1 tablespoon freshly chopped lovage,

tarragon and chervil

4 tablespoons red wine vinegar

Salt · Pepper

1. Fry the oxtail on all sides and the bacon in about 3 tablespoons of olive oil. Peel the carrots and celery and cut into pieces, peel the onion and slice. Put everything in with the oxtail and add a good 1 1/2 quarts of red wine. Stir in the tomato paste, bring to a boil and scoop off the froth.

2. Add the thyme, rosemary, cloves, peppercorns and the unpeeled garlic cloves, cover and cook for about 4 hours until the meat separates from the bones.

3. Peel two-thirds of the potatoes and cut into small pieces. Boil in salted water with caraway until tender. Strain.

4. Mash the potatoes in the potato masher, stir in warm milk, 1 to 1 1/2 oz butter and a little olive oil to form a puree.

5. Clean the mushrooms and chop. Sauté with a finely chopped shallot in 1 oz butter. Season with salt, pepper and mix with chopped herbs.

6. Strain the oxtail, save the stock and remove the fat. Preheat the oven to 480 °F.

7. Place six metal rings in a buttered pan. Peel the remaining potatoes, cut into very fine slices and lay them in the rings. Spread half of the potato puree on them and lay the boned oxtail on the puree. Distribute the mushroom ragout over this and finish with the remaining puree. Bake in the preheated oven for 1/4 hour.

8. Peel the remaining shallots, chop and sauté in 1 oz butter. Pour in the vinegar and the remaining red wine. Add the oxtail stock and boil quickly to reduce, season with salt and pepper.

9. Take the oxtail out of the rings, turn out onto plates and serve with the wine sauce.

K. and R. Obauer

If no small metal rings are available, the oxtail can also be prepared in the same way in a cake tin with an 8 inches in diameter.

Pork Fillet with Vinegar Capers and Roux Potatoes

Ingredients for 4 servings

1 1/4 lb pork fillet

15 3/4 oz firm potatoes

1/2 onion

5 tablespoons drippings

1 tablespoon flour

1/2 cup pickle juice

1 1/2 cups beef or chicken soup

1 bay leaf

4 pickles

2 tablespoons vinegar

Crushed black pepper

1 teaspoon dried marjoram

2 tablespoons butter

1 dash of oil

2 tablespoons capers in vinegar

1 clove of garlic

White wine

A dash of soy sauce (optional)

1/2 tablespoon tarragon mustard

Salt · Pepper

1. Peel the potatoes, cut into slices 1/5 inch thick.

2. Finely cut the onion and sauté in drippings. Dust with flour and roast into a roux. Pour in the pickle juice and the beef stock, season with salt and pepper and add the bay leaf. Put in the potatoes and cook until soft (about 35 minutes).

3. Cut the pickles into fine slices. Stir in the pickles, vinegar, crushed pepper and dried marjoram.

4. Trim the pork fillet, cut into slices twice as thick as the thumb and season with pepper.

5. Melt the butter and oil in a pan and fry the medaillons on both sides. Add the capers and the peeled and crushed garlic clove. Cover and braise for 5 minutes.

6. Take the meat and capers out of the pan and keep warm.

7. Pour white wine and possibly a dash of soy sauce into the pan to deglaze the brown residue. Stir in the tarragon mustard and whisk the sauce. Pour through a sieve and season with salt and pepper. Serve the pork medaillons with the capers, sauce and roux potatoes.

K. and R. Obauer

Roux potatoes and all other ragout dishes that tend to burn are best cooked in a wide enameled pot. If the pot is too high, the cooking time will be longer and the food will tend to burn.

Tasty Beef Fillet

Ingredients for 4 servings

2 lb fillet of beef (best: the middle piece)

2 tablespoons butter

2 tablespoons oil

Pepper

For the herb butter:

4 1/2 oz butter

1/2 onion

Freshly chopped herbs (e.g. 1 teaspoon of each: parsley, dill, tarragon and lovage, thyme and rosemary)

1 teaspoon capers

1 untreated lemon

1 pinch of coarsely ground pepper

1 pinch of paprika powder

1 squeeze of anchovy paste

1 clove of garlic

1 tablespoon mustard

1/2 tablespoon Worcester sauce

1 dash of cognac

2 tablespoons sour cream

1 tablespoon fresh cream

1 tablespoon crème fraîche

Salt · Pepper

1. For the herb butter: Beat the butter until creamy. Peel the onion and dice very finely. Chop all herbs very finely. Chop the capers, grate off the lemon zest.

2. Mix together the butter, onion, herbs, capers, lemon zest, crushed pepper, paprika powder, anchovy paste, the peeled and crushed clove of garlic, the mustard, Worcester sauce, cognac, sour cream, fresh cream and crème fraîche.

3. Preheat the oven to 430 °F. Pepper the meat and fry on all sides in butter and oil. Roast in the preheated oven for 20 to 25 minutes.

4. Take the meat out of the oven and pour off the fat. Put the herb butter into the dish and turn the meat in it so that the meat is coated by the butter on all sides.

5. Cut the meat into slices, arrange on plates and pour over the butter left in the dish.

K. and R. Obauer

This herb butter can also be used for pork fillet, pork medaillons or turkey breast (cooked in a piece). Noodles, polenta, gnocchi or french fries go well with this dish.

Jugged Hare in Wormwood Sauce

Ingredients for 4 servings

Fillets from the back of 1 hare

1 hare leg with the bone

6 garlic bulbs

4 carrots

1/2 shallot

3 tablespoons blueberries

3 tablespoons cranberries

1 piece of ham rind

Generous 2 quarts red wine

1 teaspoon ginger

2 teaspoons dark chocolate

1 clove

1 teaspoon dried porcini

1 pinch of dried wormwood

1 sprig of wild marjoram

1 sprig of wild mint

1 sprig of thyme

5 juniper berries

1/2 cup hare blood

Butter to thicken the sauce

1 to 2 tablespoons olive oil

Salt · Pepper

1. Cut the meat from the hare leg into large pieces, halve the garlic bulbs, peel the carrots and shallot and chop.

2. Put all ingredients into a bowl (except for the fillets, blood, butter, olive oil and salt) and marinate the meat for two days.

3. Boil the meat, the marinade and the ingredients for 1 hour. Lift the meat from the liquid and reduce the stock to half. Pour through a sieve and thicken with hare blood.

4. Mix in enough butter to produce a light, creamy sauce. Season with salt and pepper. Put the pieces of hare leg into the finished sauce.

5. Season the hare fillets with salt and pepper and sear in olive oil.

6. Serve the jugged hare with the fillets.

K. and R. Obauer

Polenta noodles, quince paste, chestnut puree or potato noodles (see recipe on page 87) go well with this.

Home Cooking

RUSTIC FEASTS

Stuffed Chinese Cabbage with Caper and Mustard Sauce

Ingredients for 4 servings

2 stale white rolls

Almost 1 cup fresh cream

2 thin Chinese cabbage heads, about 12 inches long

11 oz ground spare rib

1 egg

2 tablespoons mustard

5 tablespoons pumpkin-seed oil

1 teaspoon freshly chopped marjoram

1 pinch of ground caraway

1 clove of garlic

4 to 6 cups beef soup

2 tablespoons butter

1 tablespoon capers

4 tablespoons tarragon mustard

1/2 cup crème fraîche

Salt

Pepper

1. Soak the rolls in the fresh cream. Slit the cabbage heads lengthways to the core, pull out a few inner leaves and chop finely.

2. Take the rolls out of the cream and squeeze. Mix the ground meat with the rolls, egg, chopped cabbage, salt, pepper, mustard, pumpkin-seed oil, marjoram, caraway and the peeled and crushed garlic.

3. Fill the cabbages with the mixture, press the heads of cabbage together again, wrap in cloth napkins and tie up firmly. Put the cabbage heads into a suitable pot and pour in enough soup to cover them. Add the butter and simmer the cabbage for 45 minutes.

4. Lift the heads of cabbage out of the stock and keep warm for 10 minutes (leave them in the napkins).

5. For the sauce: Take 1 generous cup of the stock, add the capers, tarragon mustard and crème fraîche and puree with a hand blender.

6. Unwrap the cabbage heads, cut into pieces and serve in soup dishes with the sauce.

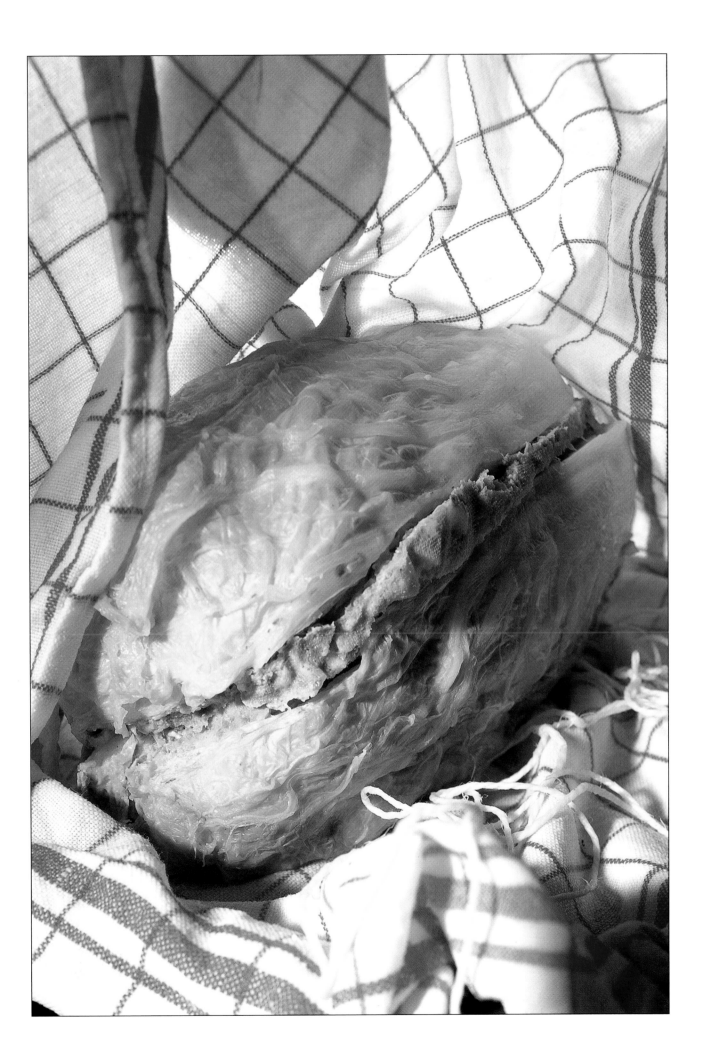

Hash Dumplings with Sausage and Turnip Kraut

Ingredients for 4 servings

Boiled beef and fried pork, a total of about 9 oz

1/2 onion

1 teaspoon dried marjoram

2 tablespoons butter

2 cloves of garlic

14 oz diced white bread (or 6 diced stale rolls)

1 pinch ground caraway

A few dried porcini, finely ground (optional)

3 tablespoons freshly chopped herbs

(e.g. parsley, chervil, chives)

4 tablespoons flour

1 cup milk

1 egg

Generous 2 quarts beef soup

7 oz Frankfurters

Salt

Pepper

For the turnip kraut:

1 lb garden turnip

A few dashes of vinegar

2 tablespoons sour cream and/or

1 tablespoon shallots

Salt

1. For the turnip kraut: Peel the turnips, grate finely, mix with salt and a few dashes of vinegar and allow to stand for about 1 hour.

2. Cut the meat into small pieces and grind.

3. Peel and chop the onion finely and sauté with the marjoram in the butter with 2 peeled and crushed cloves of garlic.

4. Mix the ground meat, sautéed onions, bread, salt, pepper, caraway, perhaps a little ground porcini powder, herbs and flour in a large bowl.

5. Boil the milk, pour over the mixture, mix in the egg, press together and allow to stand for about 1/2 hour.

6. Flour your hands, form dumplings from the mixture and simmer these in beef soup for about 10 minutes.

7. Cut the Frankfurter into slices as thick as a thumb. Just before the dumplings are ready, add these to the soup and warm them.

8. Squeeze the turnip and mix with sour cream and/or shallots.

9. Take the hash dumplings out of the soup and serve with the turnip kraut.

K. and R. Obauer

Sauerkraut can be eaten with hash dumplings instead of turnips. The dumplings can also be served in the soup. In this case, no additional accompaniment is required.

Bean Stew with Cured Ham

Ingredients for 4 servings

1/4 lb dried beans (best: scarlet runner beans,

horse beans or kidney beans)

1 lb cured, smoked ham

3 large onions · 10 cloves of garlic

6 shiitake mushrooms

5 tomatoes · 2 celery stalks

1 dried chili pepper

1/2 cup olive oil

1 bay leaf · A little savory

2 oz salami (thick slices)

2 cups beef soup

1 dash of vinegar (best: sherry vinegar)

1 to 2 teaspoons freshly chopped marjoram

Salt · Pepper

1. Soak the beans overnight in water.

2. Cut the ham into strips, slices or cubes. Peel the onions and chop coarsely. Peel the garlic, slice the garlic and mushrooms finely. Cut the tomatoes into quarters, cut the celery and chili pepper into small pieces.

3. Strain the beans. Sauté the ham in the garlic and olive oil. Add the beans, onions, tomatoes, celery, chili pepper, bay leaf, savory and salami. Pour in soup so that the liquid is twice as high as the vegetables and meat. Simmer for about 1 hour.

4. Add the mushrooms. Season the stew with salt, pepper and vinegar. Sprinkle with fresh marjoram and serve.

Cheese Dumplings

Ingredients for 4 servings

4 stale rolls

2 eggs

1/2 cup milk

3 1/2 oz Tilsit cheese

3 1/2 oz cheese from soured milk

1 onion

1 pinch grated nutmeg

1 teaspoon flour

1 to 2 tablespoons chives

1 to 2 teaspoons freshly chopped lovage

Generous 4 cups beef soup

Butter and oil for frying

Salt

Pepper

1. Cut the bread into small cubes. Mix the egg and milk with a fork. Cut both cheeses into small cubes. Peel the onion, chop finely and sauté in a little butter.

2. Mix the bread with the cheese, onion, salt, pepper, grated nutmeg and 1 teaspoon of flour. Pour the eggs and milk over this and mix. Press the mixture together and allow to stand.

3. Form small round balls and fry in half butter, half oil for 2 to 3 minutes until brown. Turn the dumplings over, cover and again fry for 2 to 3 minutes.

4. Warm the soup and ladle into dishes. Put in the cheese dumplings, sprinkle with chives and lovage and serve.

K. and R. Obauer

The dumplings are even more interesting if a handful of young nettle leaves are scalded, chopped finely and added to the dumpling mixture.

Soaked Calf's Tongue with Okra

Ingredients for 4 servings

2 calves' tongues, a total of about 1 1/2 lb

1 carrot

2 onions

2 cloves

1 pinch of ground coriander

1/2 bay leaf

1 small piece of cinnamon

7 oz okra

4 beef tomatoes

2 celery stalks

1 red bell pepper

5 1/2 oz mushrooms

7 oz small, firm potatoes

6 tablespoons olive oil

3 cloves of garlic

1 pinch of cayenne pepper

1/2 teaspoon turmeric

1 tablespoon tomato paste

1/2 cup white wine

A little cornstarch (optional)

3 tablespoons freshly chopped herbs

(e.g. chervil, chives, tarragon, hyssop)

Salt

Pepper

1. Put the calves' tongues into cold water with the carrot, a peeled onion, cloves, coriander, bay leaf and cinnamon, cover and simmer for about 2 1/2 hours until the tongue is tender at the tip. Remove the tongue from the stock and lay in cold water. Put the stock aside.

2. Wash the okra in water and halve lengthways. Slit the tomatoes and lay briefly in boiling water. Rinse with cold water, skin, remove the core and cut into quarters. Cut the celery into pieces almost 1 inch long, halve the red pepper, remove the core and cut into strips. Peel the second onion and cut into segments. Clean and quarter the mushrooms. Peel the potatoes and cut into nut-sized pieces.

3. Heat the olive oil and sauté the onions and potatoes. Stir in the remaining vegetables, peeled and crushed garlic, cayenne pepper, turmeric and tomato paste. Pour in the white wine and 1/2 cup of stock. Simmer the vegetables for 20 minutes.

4. Add the okra and simmer the vegetables for another minute, season with salt and pepper. Thicken the liquid with a little cornstarch dissolved in water if necessary.

5. Skin the tongues. Trim the thick ends, cut each into four slices lengthways and warm on the vegetables.

6. Serve the tongue on the vegetables, season with salt, pepper and chopped herbs.

Blood Sausage Ravioli with Barley and Beer Vinegar

Ingredients for 4 servings

For the ravioli:	3 tablespoons rolled barley
14 oz noodle dough (see page 23)	1 bay leaf
14 oz blood sausage	1 clove
Generous 4 cups stock from cured, smoked ham	5 peppercorns
2 tablespoons chopped chives	1 teaspoon caraway
1 tablespoon chopped lovage	1 lb sauerkraut
For the barley:	1 potato
1 small onion	Pumpkin-seed oil
1 clove of garlic	Salt · Pepper
1 tablespoon pork drippings	For the beer vinegar:
1 teaspoon sugar	1/2 cup balsamic vinegar
1/2 cup white wine (Riesling)	1/4 cup dark beer
1 generous cup beef stock or stock from cured, smoked ham	

1. For the barley: Peel the onion and cut into small cubes, peel the garlic and cut into thin slices. Heat the drippings with the sugar until golden, pour in white wine and beef or ham stock. Add the rolled barley and allow to stand for 15 minutes.

2. Wrap the spices in a cloth napkin and put in with the barley. Add the sauerkraut to the barley and simmer again for 30 minutes. Finely grate the potatoes and mix in. Season with salt and pepper.

3. Roll the noodle dough into a rectangle. Cut the blood sausage into finger-thick slices. Lay the sausage slices over half of the pastry at intervals of 1 1/2 inches. Fold the other half over the top. Cut out the ravioli and press the edges down firmly.

4. Boil the blood sausage ravioli for 5 minutes in salted water or ham stock.

5. For the beer vinegar: Mix the balsamic vinegar and the beer. Arrange the barley on four plates, lay the blood sausage ravioli on top, pour over pumpkin oil and beer vinegar and sprinkle with chives and chopped lovage.

K. and R. Obauer

Pork hock can be used to fill the ravioli instead of blood sausage.

Cheese Spaetzle

Ingredients for 4 servings

11 oz fine flour
3 eggs
1 pinch of grated nutmeg
A little milk
3 1/2 oz spicy hard cheese
2 oz Tilsit cheese
2 oz Gruyère cheese
4 tablespoons butter
1 to 2 tablespoons chopped chives
1 to 2 teaspoons freshly chopped lovage
Salt
Pepper

1. Beat the flour, eggs, grated nutmeg and a ladle of milk with a wooden spoon into a firm dough; it should stretch like chewing-gum.

2. Grate the cheese.

3. Spread the dough onto a wooden board and use a sharp knife to scratch off thin strips into salted boiling water. Boil the spaetzle for a few minutes until they float to the top and strain.

4. Heat 2 ladles of the boiling water and 1 ladle of milk. Melt the cheese in this and mix with the spaetzle.

5. Heat the butter until slightly brown. Put the cheese spaetzle into soup dishes, pour over brown butter and sprinkle with chives and lovage. If desired, season with salt and pepper.

Stuffed Potato Dumplings with Radish or Asparagus Salad

Ingredients for 6 servings

5 1/2 oz boiled beef

5 1/2 oz boiled cured and smoked ham

1 onion

A few chopped cracklings (optional)

2 tablespoons butter

1 to 2 teaspoons freshly chopped

marjoram leaves

1 lb mealy potatoes

Just over 5 1/2 oz finely ground flour

1 egg

2 tablespoons melted butter

1 pinch of grated nutmeg

A little freshly chopped lovage

Salt

Pepper

For the radish salad:

2 black radishes (or daikon)

1 dash of vinegar

2 tablespoons sour cream

Salt

For the asparagus salad:

1 bunch of asparagus

1 egg

1 dash of cider vinegar

3 to 4 tablespoons peanut oil

3 tablespoons freshly chopped herbs

(e.g. cress, basil, oregano, chervil)

A little sugar · Salt

1. Peel the onion and chop with the beef and ham. Sauté in butter, with the cracklings, if desired, and stir in the marjoram. Allow to cool.

2. Boil the potatoes in their skins, peel, and mash with the potato masher while still warm. Knead in flour, the egg, melted butter, nutmeg, salt and pepper and form into a dough.

3. Form the dough into a roll of about 2 inches in thickness and cut into slices 1/5 inch thick. Press the slices flat in the palms of the hands and cover with the filling. Close the dough over the filling to form dumplings.

4. Simmer the dumplings in water or in soup for about 8 minutes, if desired, add a piece of ham rind to the water. Remove the dumplings and arrange on plates. Sprinkle with brown butter or, better still, with pork gravy and chopped lovage.

5. For the radish salad: Peel the radishes, grate finely, salt and allow to stand for 1/4 hour.

6. Pour off the liquid, squeeze the grated radish and mix with vinegar and sour cream.

7. For the asparagus salad: Peel the asparagus, cut off the woody ends and boil in slightly salted and slightly sugared water until done. Lift out of the water, rinse with cold water and cut into pieces about 3/4 inch long.

8. Boil the egg hard, peel and grate. Measure 1/2 cup of asparagus water and mix with the grated egg, cider vinegar, peanut oil, 1 teaspoon sugar and lots of fresh herbs.

9. Mix the asparagus pieces with the marinade.

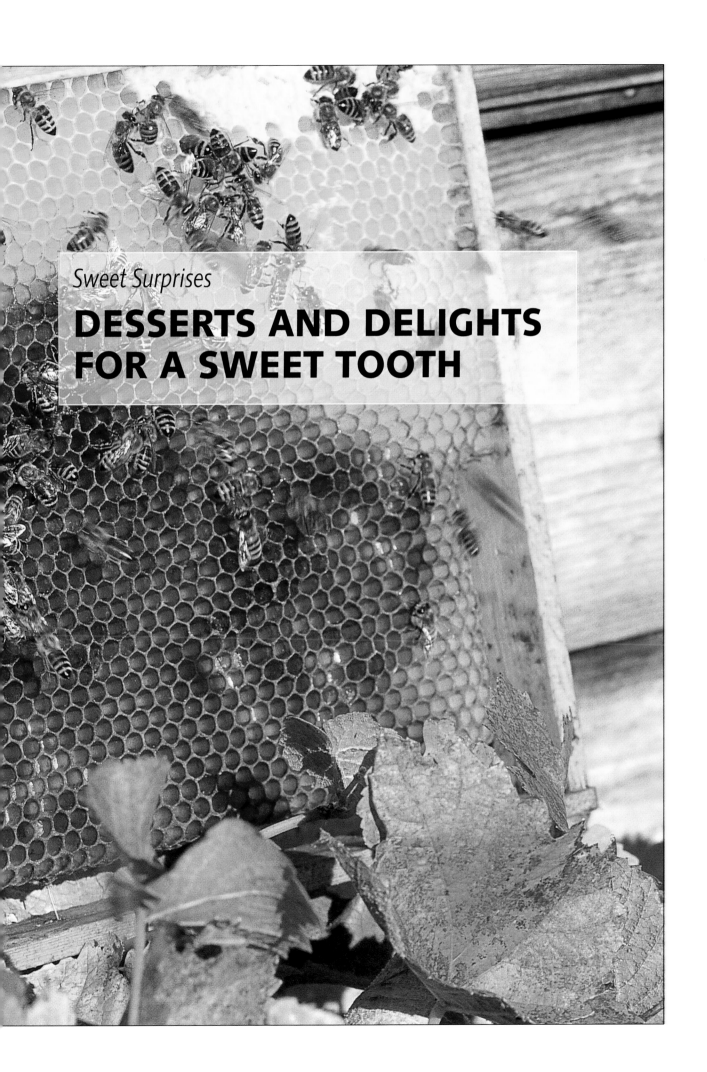

Sweet Surprises

DESSERTS AND DELIGHTS
FOR A SWEET TOOTH

Blueberry Gnocchi

Ingredients for 4 servings

1 lb blueberries

7 oz finely ground flour

1 pinch of salt

Not quite 1 cup of milk

2 tablespoons clarified butter

Sifted confectioner's sugar and sugar for dusting

1. Mix the blueberries with the flour and a pinch of salt. Stir continually while adding enough boiling milk to form a tough consistency.

2. Heat the butter fat in a large pan. Put the gnocchi mixture in spoonfuls into the pan and fry. Turn the gnocchi over. Put the lid on the pan and fry the gnocchi for a few more minutes.

3. Dust with refined and confectioner's sugar and serve. The ideal drink with these is milk.

Beer Ice Cream

Ingredients for 10 persons

6 eggs

1 dessertspoon honey

3 1/2 oz sugar

Generous 2 cups of dark beer

1/2 cup fresh cream

1. Separate the eggs. Mix the egg yolks well with honey and sugar in a blender until creamy.

2. Boil the beer. Quickly mix 1 ladle of beer with the mixture then put it into the remaining beer and heat to 172 °F (see below). Put the pot in cold water and allow to cool.

3. Stir in the cream and freeze in an ice-cream maker.

K. and R. Obauer

This goes well with prunes or baked apple wheels (see page 164). If no thermometer is at hand, do the wooden-spoon test: Dip a wooden spoon briefly into the egg mixture and blow the cream stuck to it. If it flows apart like a rose, the cream is ready. Do not heat too much or the eggs will set.

Sponge Roulade with Orange Cream

Ingredients for 8 servings

5 eggs

4 oz sugar

1 pinch of salt

4 oz finely ground flour

4 tablespoons strong coffee

9 oz mascarpone

5 1/2 oz sour cream

8 tablespoons orange marmalade

4 tablespoons orange liqueur (e. g. Grand Marnier)

White chocolate to garnish

1. Whisk the eggs with the sugar and a pinch of salt in a bowl standing over a pan of hot water until it is light and creamy. Take the bowl out of the pan of hot water and continue to whisk until it has completely cooled. Preheat the oven to 350 °F.

2. Gradually fold in the flour with a spoon. Grease and line a baking sheet, spread the mixture on this about 1/2 inch high and bake in the oven until golden brown.

3. Take the sponge out of the oven and turn out onto a sheet of greaseproof paper sprinkled with sugar. Remove the paper (wipe with a damp cloth first).

4. Sprinkle the sponge with cold coffee and roll up with the aid of the other paper.

5. Mix the mascarpone and sour cream with the orange marmalade and orange liqueur.

6. Unroll the sponge, spread with the cream and roll up again. Cover the roulade with the cream and generously scatter chips of white chocolate over it. To make these, scrape a bar of chocolate with a knife.

Curd and Lemon Cream

Ingredients for 10 portions

3 pieces of gelatin

3/4 cup milk

1 1/2 cups fresh cream

3 lemons

12 oz curds (20% fat content)

3 1/2 oz confectioner's sugar

Fruits and berries

For the sauce:

Juice of 10 lemons

About 4 tablespoons water

5 tablespoons sugar

1 teaspoon cornstarch

1. Soak the gelatin in water, squeeze well. Warm the milk and dissolve the gelatin. Whip the cream and squeeze the lemons.

2. Mix the curds with sugar, lemon juice, gelatin milk and the zest of 1 lemon. Fold in the whipped cream and stand in a cool place.

3. For the sauce: Mix the lemon juice with a little water and sugar. Dissolve a little cornstarch in a little water, add to this and bring to a boil until the sauce thickens.

4. Take out scoops of the cream and serve with lemon sauce, fruit and berries.

Dried Pear and Poppy Seed Strudel

Ingredients for 12 portions

9 oz frozen strudel pastry (2 sheets)

Butter

For the filling:

9 oz dried pears

1 generous cup white wine

2 cups milk

2 oz butter

3 1/2 oz sugar

2 oz honey

1 teaspoon ground cinnamon

Zest of 1 untreated lemon

Contents of 1 vanilla pod

14 oz ground poppy seed

5 1/2 oz breadcrumbs

For the milk:

1 generous cup milk

2 oz sugar

1/2 oz vanilla sugar

2 eggs

2 egg yolks

4 tablespoons advocaat

1. For the filling: chop the dried pears and soak in the wine. Boil the milk with the butter, sugar, honey, cinnamon, lemon zest and the contents of the vanilla pod. Stir in the poppy seed and breadcrumbs and allow to cook a little. Stir in the pears.

2. Thinly roll out the two sheets of strudel pastry. Spread the filling on the pastry. Roll up the two sheets of pastry and close the ends.

3. Butter an ovenproof dish with high sides. Lay the strudel in this and brush with melted butter.

4. For the milk: Warm 1/2 cup milk and melt the sugar and vanilla sugar in it. Mix the remaining milk, the eggs, yolks and advocaat and stir into the sugared milk, but do not allow to boil.

5. Pour this milk over the strudel which must be well covered. Bake the strudel for about 1/2 hour at 390 °F.

6. Allow the strudel to cool a little before cutting into portions. Vanilla ice cream goes well with this.

Gugelhupf

Ingredients for 1 Gugelhupf

3 eggs

1 generous cup fresh cream

1 teaspoon vanilla sugar

9 oz sugar

9 oz finely ground flour

2 teaspoons baking powder

3 tablespoons milk

3 tablespoons nougat cream

Butter and flour for the mold

1. Separate the eggs. Whip the cream until fluffy but not stiff. Continue whisking and add the sugar and vanilla sugar. Mix in the yolks. Fold in the flour and baking powder and add the milk.

2. Beat the egg whites until stiff and fold in. Mix the nougat cream into a third of the quantity.

3. Butter a ring-shaped mold and dust with flour. First put in the nougat third, then add the rest of the mixture.

4. Bake the Gugelhupf for about 1 hour at 360 °F.

Apple Strudel with Sour Cream

Ingredients for 6 to 8 servings

For the pastry:

9 oz finely ground flour

1 to 2 tablespoons oil

1 pinch of salt · About 2 teaspoons warm water

For the filling:

8 to 10 medium-sized, not so sweet apples

3 tablespoons sugar

2 tablespoons raisins

3 tablespoons ground nuts

Juice of 1 lemon

1/2 teaspoon ground cinnamon

For the breadcrumbs:

2 oz butter

Just over 2 oz breadcrumbs

Also:

About 3 1/2 oz melted butter for the baking tin

and for brushing

9 oz sour cream

1. Knead the ingredients for the pastry on a board without flour until the sticky tough pastry becomes silky smooth and soft and no longer sticks to the board and the hands. Sprinkle the pastry with flour, cover with transparent foil and leave to stand in a warm place for about 1/2 hour.

2. For the filling: Peel and core the apples and cut into thick slices. Mix with the remaining ingredients for the filling. Allow the filling to stand for about 10 minutes.

3. For the breadcrumbs: Heat the butter and roast the breadcrumbs in it until light.

4. Roll the pastry out with a rolling pin on a floured cloth as far as possible. Use the back of the hand to then stretch the pastry from the middle until it is as thin as paper (spread oil on your hands) and form it into a rectangle. Pre-heat the oven to 390°F.

5. Spread the breadcrumbs lengthways over one-third of the pastry and spread the filling on the breadcrumbs. Leave about 4 inches along the side free so that the pastry can be easily wrapped over. Brush the remaining part of the pastry with melted butter and cut off any thick edges. Lift the cloth on the side with the filling and roll the pastry up towards the side with no filling. Press the edges down firmly.

6. Brush a cake tin, that is just the right size and not too big, with butter. Use the cloth to lift the strudel into the tin. Brush with butter and bake in the preheated oven for 35 to 40 minutes. Brush continually while baking with the butter and the juice formed from the filling.

7. Allow the strudel to cool a little after baking. Cut into portions with a serrated knife, sprinkle with sugar and serve with sour cream.

K. and R. Obauer

When the strudel pastry is being stretched, close all doors and windows and make sure the room temperature is normal, otherwise the pastry could become tough and brittle. The baking tin should not be too large or the strudel will lose its shape.

Blueberry Schmarren

Ingredients for 2 main courses or 4 desserts

9 oz coarsely ground flour

1 pinch salt

1 generous cup milk

4 eggs

2 tablespoons clarified butter

1 tablespoon butter

3 1/2 oz blueberries

Sugar as desired

1. Mix the flour with a pinch of salt and the cold milk to a thick consistency. Briefly mix in the eggs, but not completely.

2. Melt the clarified butter and butter in a large pan. Pour in the mixture, cover and cook at a moderate heat. The pancake has to rise at the sides.

3. Make criss-cross cuts in the pancake with a knife, turn and fry until almost ready. Rip into pieces with two forks.

4. Add the blueberries and sugar as desired. Cover the pan again and fry the Schmarren for a few more minutes.

K. and R. Obauer

Do not pour too much pancake mix into the pan! The Schmarren turns out best when it has plenty of room to expand.

Cinnamon Dumplings with Apricot Ragout

Ingredients for 4 servings

For the dumplings:

1 generous cup milk

1 clove · 1 pinch ground cinnamon

1 pinch of salt

3 1/2 oz semolina · 1 egg

Cinnamon sugar (2 tablespoons sugar and

1/2 teaspoon cinnamon)

Confectioner's sugar for dusting

A few mint leaves to garnish

For the apricot ragout:

3 1/4 lb apricots · 1/2 cup white wine

2 tablespoons apricot brandy

2 spoons of sugar (to taste)

Also: Generous 4 cups milk for boiling.

1. Wash, stone and quarter the apricots. Boil two-thirds of the apricots with the wine and apricot brandy, add sugar and puree in the blender. Press through a sieve.

2. Put the remaining apricots into a jar with a lid. Pour the hot apricot puree over them. Close the jar and allow the apricot ragout to cool.

3. Bring the milk, clove, cinnamon and salt to a boil. Add the semolina and cook for 15 minutes while continually stirring. Allow to cool and stir in the egg.

4. Make 12 small dumplings from the dough. Allow the dumplings to steep in the hot milk for about 5 minutes. They are ready when they float to the top.

5. Toss the dumplings in cinnamon sugar and serve with the apricot ragout. Dust with confectioner's sugar and garnish with mint.

Salzburg Gnocchi

Ingredients for 4 servings

2 tablespoons milk

1 1/2 oz butter

8 tablespoons sugar

1/2 teaspoons vanilla sugar

4 tablespoons almond milk or Amaretto

8 egg whites

2 tablespoons coarsely ground flour

Zest of 1/2 untreated lemon

6 egg yolks

2 oz marzipan

Confectioner's sugar

1. Distribute the milk, butter, 2 tablespoons of sugar, vanilla sugar and almond milk in two oval porcelain molds (12 x 6 x 1 1/2 inches) and allow to caramelize on the stove.

2. Whisk the egg whites with the remaining sugar until stiff. Fold the flour, grated lemon zest and egg yolks into the whisked egg whites and stir quickly two or three times.

3. Put a part of this mixture into the molds (about 1/2 inch high). Cut the marzipan into thin slices and put on top.

4. Quickly scoop small gnocchi out of the remaining mixture and put into the molds. Bake the gnocchi for about 1/4 hour at 370 to 390 °F.

5. Scoop the gnocchi out of the molds and put on plates. Dust with confectioner's sugar and serve with fruit sauce, vanilla sauce and fruit or compote.

Nut Macaroons

Ingredients for 40 pieces

3 egg whites

9 3/4 oz sugar

Juice and zest of 1/2 untreated lemon

9 3/4 oz ground walnuts

40 round paper-thin wafers with a diameter

of 1 1/2 inches

For the cream:

4 oz butter

3 1/2 oz confectioner's sugar

3 1/2 oz baker's chocolate or bitter chocolate

1 egg (optional)

For the icing:

9 oz baker's chocolate or bitter chocolate

coating

9 oz butter

1. Whisk the egg whites, sugar, grated lemon zest and lemon juice until stiff. Fold in the nuts.

2. Lay the wafers on a baking sheet and spoon the macaroon mixture onto the wafers in small heaps. Bake for about 15 minutes at 350 to 390 °F until the mixture is almost dry inside.

3. For the cream: Whisk the butter with the sugar. Melt the chocolate over hot water or in the microwave oven and fold into the whisked butter. If desired, mix in 1 egg.

4. Allow the macaroons to cool and then spread butter cream on them. Put the macaroons in a cool place until the cream has set.

5. For the icing: Melt the chocolate and stir in the butter. Dip the macaroons into the icing (except for the bottom) and allow to set.

Rice Soufflé with Raspberry Chaudeau

Ingredients for 8 servings
(For a 11 1/2 x 7 inches tin)

2 oz long-grained rice

1/2 cup milk

1 tablespoon butter

3 eggs

1/2 oz confectioner's sugar

1/2 oz sugar

Breadcrumbs

For the meringue topping:

2 egg whites

3 1/2 oz sugar

2 tablespoons grated coconut

For the raspberry chaudeau:

2 tablespoons pureed raspberries

2 egg yolks

3 tablespoons white wine

1 tablespoon raspberry schnapps

2 teaspoons vanilla sugar

1. Cook the rice with the milk and butter and allow to cool.

2. Separate the eggs. Whisk the yolks with the confectioner's sugar until creamy, whisk the egg whites with the sugar until stiff. Carefully fold the beaten whites and yolks into the rice.

3. Brush a mold with butter and sprinkle with breadcrumbs. Pour in the mixture and bake for about 30 minutes at 410 °F.

4. For the meringue topping: whisk the egg whites with sugar until stiff. Use an icing bag to pipe the meringue mixture onto the baked rice soufflé and sprinkle over grated coconut. Bake the rice in the oven again for 5 to 10 minutes at a high temperature.

5. For the chaudeau: Whisk all ingredients in a bowl standing in a pan of hot water until creamy. Serve the chaudeau with the rice soufflé immediately.

K. and R. Obauer

*The rice soufflé tastes very good if made with
steamed pears or drained pear compote.
To do this, put half of the rice mixture into
the mold, put in the pears, cover with the rest
of the rice mixture.
Try this with some vanilla ice cream.*

Walnut Cake

Ingredients for 1 cake with a diameter of 8 inches

For the dough:

5 1/2 oz cold butter

2 1/2 oz confectioner's sugar

7 oz flour · 5 1/2 oz sugar

3 1/2 oz chopped walnuts

For the nut filling:

1 tablespoon butter · 4 eggs

2 oz confectioner's sugar

1 1/2 oz sweet baking chocolate

3 1/2 oz ground walnuts

For the icing:

2 tablespoons walnut liqueur

1 oz confectioner's sugar

1. Quickly combine the ingredients for the dough and knead them together. Wrap the dough in plastic wrap and let it rest in a cool place.

2. Roll the pastry out to about 1 tenth of an inch. Cut out a circle 8 inches across and cover the bottom of a greased springform tin. Prick several times with a fork. Bake the bottom blind for about 10 minutes at 390 °F (To do this, lay greaseproof paper on the bottom, cover with dried pulses and remove these after baking).

3. Put 2 oz sugar into a pan and heat while stirring until it becomes light brown. Stir in the chopped walnuts and the butter. Allow the walnuts to cool in the butter.

4. Melt the sweet baking chocolate in a bain-marie. Mix the coating, ground and caramelized nuts with the egg yolk mixture. Fold in the whisked egg whites.

5. Spread the nut mixture on the prebaked crust and bake the cake for about 45 minutes at 350 °F.

6. For the icing: mix the sugar with liqueur and spread on the cake while warm.

Coffee Blancmange

Ingredients for 18 molds, each about 1/3 cup

9 oz sugar

2 cups coffee

2 oz cocoa

2 tablespoons Amaretto

2 tablespoons orange liqueur (e. g. Grand Marnier)

1 generous cup fresh cream

1 generous cup milk

8 egg yolks

6 eggs

For the caramel:

5 1/2 oz sugar

Not quite half a cup of water

For the orange sauce:

2 cups freshly squeezed orange juice

3 tablespoons sugar

1 dash of orange liqueur (e. g. Grand Marnier)

1 teaspoon cornstarch

1. First prepare the caramel: Boil the sugar in the water until it turns golden brown. Pour the caramel into the molds so that the bottom is well covered.

2. Heat the sugar with the coffee, cocoa, Amaretto and orange liqueur until the sugar has dissolved (do not boil). Beat the cream with the milk, yolks and eggs. Stir it into the coffee.

3. Pour the mixture into the molds and allow to stand for 10 minutes. Poach the filled molds standing in a pan of water in the oven for about 40 minutes at 300 °F. Allow to cool.

4. For the orange sauce: Bring the juice, sugar and liqueur to the boil. Dissolve a little cornstarch in a little water and thicken the juice slightly. Allow to cool.

5. Turn the blancmanges out of the molds and serve with the sauce.

K. and R. Obauer

It is important to let the mixture stand! Air is beaten in when whisking and if the blancmanges are cooked immediately, holes will form.

Ovomaltine Cake

Ingredients for 1 cake

For the meringue:

2 egg whites (2 oz)

2 oz sugar

2 oz confectioner's sugar

For the sponge:

6 eggs

5 1/2 oz sugar

5 1/2 oz flour

1 tablespoon cocoa

For the syrup:

1 1/4 cups water

2 tablespoons rum

2 tablespoons coffee liqueur or advocaat

3 1/2 oz cocoa

For the cream:

4 1/2 oz dark chocolate

4 tablespoons water

2 tablespoons advocaat

9 oz butter

2 1/2 oz cocoa

2 1/2 oz Ovomaltine

6 egg yolks

2 1/2 oz sugar

2 cups fresh cream

Currant jam for spreading

1. For the meringue: Whisk the egg whites with the refined sugar and the confectioner's sugar until very stiff. Lay greaseproof paper on a baking sheet and spread the whisked egg whites on this about 1/2 inch high. Dry in an oven at 140 °F for about half a day.

2. For the sponge: Separate the eggs. Whisk the yolks with sugar until very creamy. Whisk the egg whites until stiff. Fold the egg whites very carefully and alternately with flour and cocoa into the yolks. Spread on a baking sheet lined with greaseproof paper and bake for about 10 minutes at 350 °F.

3. For the syrup: Bring all ingredients to the boil and allow to cool.

4. For the cream: Heat the dark chocolate with the water and advocaat until the chocolate has melted. Beat the butter, cocoa and Ovomaltine until fluffy. Beat the egg yolks with sugar until creamy and stir into the cocoa mixture. Stir in the melted dark chocolate. Whip the cream until stiff and fold in.

5. Cut the meringue and the sponge each into three strips of the same width. Spread the first strip with syrup, spread the cream on top and cover with the meringue. Spread this with currant jam. Layer the remaining ingredients in the same way. Finish with cream. Put in a cool place for half a day.

Poppy Seed Cake

Ingredients for one baking sheet (about 13 x 17 inches)

8 eggs
5 1/2 oz confectioner's sugar
5 1/2 oz sugar
14 oz ground poppy seed
9 1/2 oz butter

1. Separate the eggs. Whisk the yolks with confectioner's sugar until fluffy. Beat the egg whites with sugar until stiff and mix with the yolk mixture.

2. Fold in the poppy seed. Melt 8 3/4 oz of butter (not too hot) and stir in.

3. Butter a rectangular cake tin. Pour in the mixture and bake the cake for 30 minutes at 350 °F.

K. and R. Obauer

This cake can also be topped with apple slices or peach halves.

Baked Apple Wheels

Ingredients for 4 servings

3 not so sweet, firm-fleshed apples

3 tablespoons flour

1/2 cup wine (e.g. Gewürztraminer)

1 pinch of salt · 2 eggs

1 heaping tablespoon sugar

A little flour for coating

About 1 lb clarified butter

Cinnamon sugar (1 teaspoon ground cinnamon and 2 tablespoons sugar)

For the wine chaudeau:

2 egg yolks

1/2 cup wine

2 tablespoons sugar

1. Core the apples and cut into thick slices.

2. Mix the flour, wine and a pinch of salt into a dough the consistency of a thick paste. Separate the eggs. Mix in the yolks. Whisk the egg whites with sugar until stiff and fold in.

3. Toss the apple slices in flour, dip in the batter and fry in clarified butter until golden brown.

4. Lift the apple slices out of the fat and drain on paper towel. Dust with cinnamon sugar.

5. For the wine chaudeau: Whisk the yolks, wine and sugar in a bain-marie on a not too high heat until fluffy, while continually turning the bowl (the eggs should not be heated too quickly).

Serve immediately with the apple wheels.

Milk Bread and Apricot "Sandwiches"

Ingredients for 4 servings

For the cream:

1 cup milk · 2 tablespoons sugar

1/2 teaspoon vanilla sugar

2 egg yolks

1 tablespoon vanilla pudding mix

For the sandwiches:

8 slices of milk bread (about 3/4 inch thick)

2 tablespoons apricot jam

1 lb clarified butter · 4 eggs

A little milk for dunking

1. Bring the milk to a boil, beat the sugar, vanilla sugar, egg yolks to a cream, add the milk and let the mixture boil to a cream.

2. Spread one half of the bread slices with the pudding cream and one half with apricot jam. Stick together one piece spread with the pudding cream to one spread with jam (spread sides together).

3. Heat the clarified butter. Beat the eggs. Dip the "sandwiches" briefly into milk, turn in the beaten eggs and lay in the hot fat. Fry until golden brown for 3 to 4 minutes. Turn as soon as one side is brown and baste the upper side again with fat.

4. Lift the "sandwiches" out of the fat and drain on paper towel.

K. and R. Obauer

These taste best when served with "young-wine chaudeau" as in the recipe on the left, but replace the wine with the season's new wine.

Index